HUMAN CAPITAL AT WORK

The value of experience

Prof. Marcão – Marcus Vinícius Pinto

2024

HUMAN CAPITAL AT WORK

HUMAN CAPITAL AT WORK

© **Copyright 2024 - All rights reserved.**

The information provided herein is stated to be true and consistent, wherein any liability, in terms of inattention or otherwise, for any use or abuse of any policies, processes or guidance contained herein is the sole and absolute responsibility of the reader.

Under no circumstances shall any legal liability or fault be maintained against the authors for any repair, damage or monetary loss due to the information contained herein, whether directly or indirectly.

The authors own all copyrights to this work.

Legal Issues

This book is copyrighted. This is for personal use only. You may not alter, distribute, or sell any part or the contents of this book without the consent of the authors or copyright owner. If this is violated, legal action may be initiated.

The information contained herein is offered for informational purposes only and is therefore universal. The presentation of the information is without contract or any kind of warranty.

The trademarks that are used in this book are used for examples or composition of arguments. This use is done without any consent, and the publication of the trademark is without permission or endorsement from the trademark owner and are the property of the owners themselves, not affiliated herewith.

The images that are present here without authorship citation are public domain images or were created by the authors of the book.

HUMAN CAPITAL AT WORK

Disclaimer:

Please note that the information contained in this document is for educational and entertainment purposes only. Every effort has been made to provide complete, accurate, up-to-date and reliable information. No warranty of any kind is express or implied.

By reading this text, the reader agrees that under no circumstances are the authors liable for any losses, direct or indirect, incurred as a result of the use of the information contained in this book, including, but not limited to, errors, omissions, or inaccuracies.

ISBN: 9798320829197

Selo editorial: Independently published

HUMAN CAPITAL AT WORK

Summary

1   IS KNOWLEDGE IN THE SCHOOL YEARS IMPORTANT?   21

1.1   The difficult relationship between school students and their version as professionals.   28
1.2   THE INFORMATION CHALLENGE   31

2   INFORMATION – THE RAW MATERIAL OF EVERYTHING.   44

2.1   History of Little Red Riding Hood in the headlines of major magazines and newspapers   54
2.2   The value of information   57
2.3   Information and strategic information system   62
2.4   Information and Information Retrieval Systems: genera of the same species?   66
2.5   Chaos   70
2.6   Information Science   73

3   HUMAN CAPITAL AT WORK. THE VALUE OF EXPERIENCE.   79

3.1   Work experience adds to the value of human capital   82
3.2   Work experience contributes 40 to 60% of a worker's human capital   84
3.3   The bolder the movement, the greater the momentum.   92
3.3.1   Understand the potential in people, as well as their current knowledge and skills.   96
3.3.2   Embrace mobility.   99
3.3.3   Strengthen coaching, especially at the beginning of an employee's tenure.   99

4   THE NECESSARY KNOWLEDGE THAT EVERY PROFESSIONAL IN THE MODERN WORLD SHOULD HAVE.   104

4.1	HIGHER COURSE.	107
4.2	POSTGRADUATE STUDIES.	109
4.3	IS THE PROFESSIONAL DESIRED BY COMPANIES AN ENTREPRENEUR?	113
4.4	A NETWORK ALSO INFLUENCES YOUR KNOWLEDGE.	115

5	**KNOWLEDGE. YOUR HUMAN CAPITAL.**	**121**
5.1	MEANING OF KNOWLEDGE	121
5.2	WHAT ARE THE TYPES OF KNOWLEDGE	123
5.2.1	COMMON SENSE KNOWLEDGE	123
5.2.2	THEOLOGICAL KNOWLEDGE	123
5.2.3	PHILOSOPHICAL KNOWLEDGE	124
5.2.4	SCIENTIFIC KNOWLEDGE	124
5.2.5	KNOWLEDGE FOR PHILOSOPHY	126
5.2.6	FAITH.	128
5.3	LIFE IS A SCHOOL.	131
5.4	**CAVE MYTH.**	**134**
5.4.1	WHAT DOES THE MYTH OF THE CAVE SAY?	134
5.4.2	INTERPRETATION OF THE CAVE MYTH	137
5.4.3	HOW WOULD THE MYTH OF THE CAVE FIT IN TODAY?	138
5.4.4	THE REPUBLIC, THE BOOK CONTAINING THE MYTH OF THE CAVE	140

6	**FAKE NEWS OR HOW TO DEVALUE THE IMPORTANCE OF EXPERIENCE.**	**142**
6.1	WHAT DOES FAKE NEWS MEAN?	142
6.2	HOW DOES FAKE NEWS WORK?	143
6.3	EXAMPLES AND CONSEQUENCES OF FAKE NEWS	145
6.4	HOW TO FIGHT FAKE NEWS?	146
6.5	FALSE SCIENCE CAN BE FATAL.	147
6.6	VALIDATED INFORMATION NEEDS TO BE PUT INTO PRACTICE.	148
6.7	EVOLUTION OF SCIENTIFIC VALIDATION.	149
6.8	THE CHANGING SCENARIO: THE REVOLUTION IN THE PRODUCTION OF KNOWLEDGE.	150
6.9	CONSEQUENCES FOR SCIENCE AND FOR SCIENTIFIC PUBLICATION AND EVALUATION	151
6.10	WAYS FORWARD	154
6.11	WHAT IS THE ROLE OF A LEADER IN STOPPING FAKE NEWS IN THE WORKPLACE?	157
6.12	WHAT IS MISINFORMATION IN THE WORKPLACE AND HOW TO IDENTIFY IT?	157

6.13	6 WAYS TO STOP FAKE NEWS IN THE WORKPLACE.	159
7	**SOFT SKILLS: WHAT THEY ARE, EXAMPLES AND HOW TO DEVELOP.**	**164**
7.1	WHAT ARE SOFT SKILLS?	165
7.2	EXEMPLOS DE SOFT SKILLS	165
7.3	WHAT ARE THE SOFT SKILLS MOST IN DEMAND BY COMPANIES?	166
1.1	WHAT ARE THE DIFFERENCES BETWEEN SOFT SKILLS AND HARD SKILLS?	166
7.4	WHAT IS THE IMPORTANCE OF SOFT SKILLS?	167
7.5	HOW TO ASSESS SOFT SKILLS DURING THE JOB INTERVIEW?	168
7.6	HOW TO DEVELOP SOFT SKILLS IN YOUR EMPLOYEES?	169
7.7	WHAT TOOLS CAN BE USED IN THE DEVELOPMENT OF SOFT SKILLS?	170
7.8	LEADERSHIP. THE MAIN SOFT SKILL OF THE SUCCESSFUL PROFESSIONAL.	171
8	**ANDRAGOGY – ADULT EDUCATION.**	**176**
8.1	ANDRAGOGY IN BUSINESS	181
8.2	SOME BASIC PRINCIPLES	183
8.3	HR ADMINISTRATION	185
8.4	CLASH OF GENERATIONS	186
9	**CONCLUSION.**	**189**
10	**FAQ.**	**192**
10	**REFERENCES.**	**200**
11	**MEET THE AUTHOR.**	**211**
11.1	PROF. MARCÃO - MARCUS VINÍCIUS PINTO.	211
11.2	SOME BOOKS PUBLISHED BY PROF. MARCÃO.	213
11.3	BOOKS ON OPEN DATA BY PROF. MARCÃO.	215
11.4	HOW TO CONTACT PROF. MARCÃO.	216

HUMAN CAPITAL AT WORK

Index of Illustrations.

Figure 1 - Citation by José Lima. _____ *13*
Figure 2 – Quote Aristotle - the experience. _____ *14*
Figure 3 – Mafalda and the Sick World. _____ *19*
Figure 4- The young person at the current school. _____ *21*
Figure 5 – Zygmunt Bauman. _____ *23*
Figure 6 – Bauman and the questioning. _____ *24*
Figura 7 – Marcel Gouchet. _____ *26*
Figure 8 – Is learning really useful? _____ *29*
Figura 9 - Vannevar Bush. _____ *33*
Figura 10– Science, the endless frontier. _____ *34*
Figura 11 – As we may think. _____ *35*
Figure 12 – Einstein and the questioning. _____ *37*
Figure 13 - Tim Berners-Lee. _____ *38*
Figure 14 - Information or mess? _____ *39*
Figure 15 – Growth in data production _____ *40*
Figure 16 – One minute on the Internet in 2021. _____ *41*
Figure 17 – Competencies of the IT professional. _____ *42*
Figure 18 - Is a magnifying glass useful? _____ *44*
Figure 19 – The Prague Golem. _____ *46*
Figure 20 – The Golem and the Rabbi. _____ *47*
Figure 21 – Ultron, a villain product of information. _____ *49*
Figure 22 - Tony Stark and his technological creations. _____ *49*
Figure 23 - Mickey Apprentice Sorcerer. _____ *50*
Figura 24 - Laocoön and His Sons. _____ *52*
Figure 25 - The Wolf and Little Red Riding Hood. _____ *55*
Figure 26 – Model of the relationship between supply and demand. _____ *58*
Figure 27 - Data subdivisions. _____ *60*
Figure 28 – What the data can produce. _____ *61*
Figure 29 – Organizational vs. strategic information. _____ *65*
Figure 30- Systemic Approach. _____ *69*
Figure 31 - Chaos. _____ *72*
Figure 32 – Information Science. _____ *76*
Figure 33 – Only experience enables the professional _____ *80*
Figure 34 - Shakespeare and the search for work. _____ *81*
Figure 35 - The difficult professional climb. _____ *83*

Figure 36 – The difference experience makes. _____ *88*
Figure 37 – Human capital as a professional factor. _____ *90*
Figure 38 – The dedication of the professional. _____ *91*
Figure 39 – Mafalda and the problem of right and wrong. _____ *95*
Figure 40- Access to higher education. _____ *108*
Figure 41 – Knowledge quadrant. _____ *111*
Figure 42 – Structure of hierarchical levels. _____ *112*
Figure 43 – A good network can make all the difference. _____ *116*
Figure 44 – Knowledge. _____ *121*
John Locke is an important figure in modern empiricism. _____ *127*
Figure 46 - The learning process. _____ *132*
Figure 47 - The Myth of the Cave, or Allegory of the Cave. _____ *135*
Figure 48 – A shadow on the wall. _____ *136*
Plato is one of the thinkers of Ancient Greece. _____ *137*
Figure 50 – Too much access, too little knowledge. _____ *139*
Figure 51 - Fake news is shared mainly on social networks. _____ *142*
Figure 52 - Fake news hackers usually operate in a zone of the internet called the deep web. _____ *144*
Figure 53 - The chances of fake news being passed on are much higher than those of true news. _____ *146*
Figure 54 – Fake news can generate suffering in teams. _____ *158*
Figura 55 – Soft Skills. _____ *164*
Figure 56 – Pedagogy vs andragogy. _____ *176*
Figure 57 – Andragogy. _____ *178*
Figure 58 – Andragogy. _____ *182*
Figure 59 – The Value of Human Capital. _____ *189*
Figure 60 – Dilbert and the corporate world. _____ *191*
Figure 61 - The Value of Human Capital. _____ *211*
Figure 62 – Some books by Prof. Marcão. _____ *215*
Figure 63 – Let's value teachers. _____ *217*

To my beloved Andrea,
that may not always be right,
But he's always right.
Prof. Marcão – Marcus Vinícius Pinto

HUMAN CAPITAL AT WORK

Foreword

The analysis of the value of the current professional implies discussing the enigma of the challenges that permeate the techniques and practices used in the business environment.

This book was born from my experience as an entrepreneur with the aim of serving different audiences who are looking for more than a title and content about the value of experience as a marker of employability and workability of the professional and their capacity as an entrepreneur and intrapreneur.

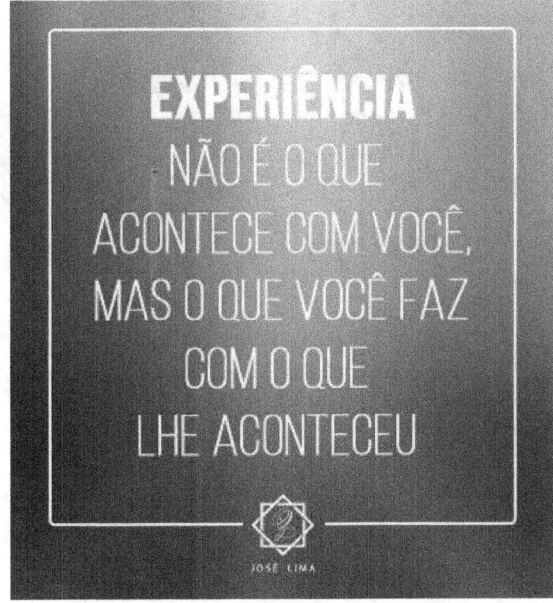

Figure 1 - Citation José Lima.

This book has several characteristics that make it a unique work for you who seek to understand how to value experience in the corporate and business world.

Firstly, it offers a technical perspective based on the observation of the dynamics of the "oil of the modern economy", information. It addresses the issue of human experience as a generator of the professional's entrepreneurial attitude. It permeates the issue of knowledge as an input for each and every activity of the human being.

It deals with an issue that compromises the value of the professional's experience: fake news. In this view, it includes soft skills as a professional differentiating factor.

The final chapters dealing with andragogy and intelligence/intelligence bring to a close the thought that will surely take your idea of being human as a hardworking and enterprising being to a level you didn't think possible.

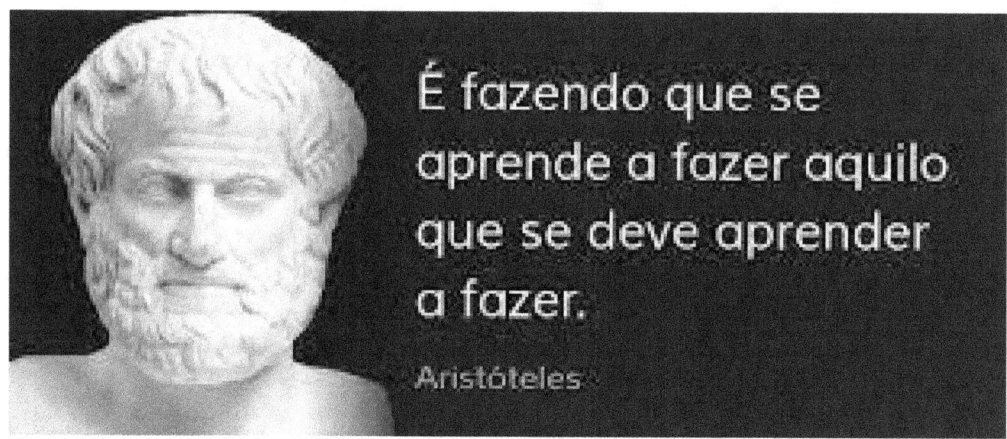

Figure 2 – Quote Aristotle – experience.

Notice that one of the by-products of this book is the parallel presented between knowledge and competence in a timely and current way, because today more than knowledge, the competence to "make it happen" is required from all professional levels towards the consolidation of positions and achievement of results.

I close this preface with two inspiring quotes from the world of management. The first comes from José Lima, who reminds us: "The analysis of the value of the current professional implies discussing the enigma of the challenges that permeate the techniques and practices used in the business environment."

And the second quote is from none other than Aristotle, who teaches us about the importance of experience: "Experience is the best teacher of all things."

Based on these reflections, I invite you to dive into this book that addresses the value of experience, knowledge as an essential input, and the competence to "make it happen" in the corporate world. Develop your entrepreneurial skills, explore soft skills, and understand how andragogy and intelligence/intelligence can elevate your professional journey to levels you never thought possible.

This book was written with the intention of serving different audiences in search of a deeper understanding of the value of experience in the business environment. Its technical and timeless perspective leads us to fundamental reflections to achieve success and solid results in the business world.

Don't miss the opportunity to acquire this unique work, which contains a timely parallel between knowledge and competence. Get ready to excel professionally and consolidate prominent positions in your career. Remember, knowledge is essential, but the competence to turn it into action is what makes us true protagonists of success.

Invest in yourself, always!

Happy reading!

Happy learning!

Prof. Marcão - Marcus Vinícius Pinto
Professor, founder, CEO and
pedagogical coordinator of MVP
Consult.

HUMAN CAPITAL AT WORK

The biggest enemies of professional growth are lack of motivation and self-indulgence.

It's when the person doesn't know where they want to go and is content to stay where they are.

Susanne Diniz

HUMAN CAPITAL AT WORK

Figure 3 – Mafalda and the Sick World.

HUMAN CAPITAL AT WORK

1 IS KNOWLEDGE IN THE SCHOOL YEARS IMPORTANT?

In recent decades, there has been a gradual expansion of access to schooling for the less favored groups of the population in Brazil, but this growth is not guaranteeing the democratization of access to knowledge that such schooling proposes to make possible.

Such a challenge is a fundamental issue when it comes to promoting the social quality of education. The issue is the quality of basic education, in the sense defended by authors such as Dourado and Oliveira (2009); Silva (2009), among others, understood from the perspective of social quality.

What do young men and women and adults think they are learning in middle school? How are technologies conveyed in this context?

Would the relationships with technologies and the recurrent learning of them be incompatible with the ways of learning in traditional schools? Are these cultural artifacts hindering school learning? Or, in another sense, are such artifacts the solutions to solve the issues of learning in school?

Figure 4- The young person at their current school.

The society of producers, for Zigmunt Bauman, is the main model of the solid phase of modernity, it was based on stable security, secure stability, discipline and subordination and was based on the routinization of individual behavior.

With the change in society's focus, which puts consumption in the foreground, the transformation of the relationship with time is identified. It is no longer apprehended as cyclical or linear, but presents itself as fragmented, or even pulverized in a multiplicity of eternal instants.

Life, whether individual or social, is nothing more than a succession of gifts, a collection of moments experienced with varying intensity.

As the author explains, in this way of understanding the world, the notion of progress, made possible by human efforts, is not valued.

> *"The idea of the time of necessity has been replaced by the concept of the time of possibilities, open at any moment, by the unpredictability of the new. What matters is the present moment, not missing the opportunity, because there would be no new chance. This haste is partly justified by the impulse to acquire things and the need to replace and discard them.*

It is believed in the possibility of buying happiness, not promised for eternal life, but accessible in earthly life. The prevailing idea is that in order to be happy, everyone needs to be, should be, and must be a consumer by vocation; It is justified that consuming is a universal human right that knows no exception.

Thus, the consumer society does not recognize age or gender differences. Nor does it recognize class distinctions. The poor begin to spend what little money they have on consumer objects to avoid exclusion, and thus fail to satisfy their basic needs.

Figure 5 – Zygmunt Bauman[1].

Subjects feel the need to consume to protect their self-esteem, so as not to feel "inadequate, deficient and substandard". Professionals, at all levels, do not escape this scenario by flaunting all kinds of consumer goods on their social networks.

For Bauman,

> "Consuming, therefore, means investing in one's social affiliation."

---

[1] Polish philosopher, sociologist, professor and writer. His work influences studies in sociology, philosophy, and psychology. He is one of the greatest intellectuals of the 21st century. While studying human interactions in late Modernity, also called Postmodernity, he realized that "relationships trickle down the space between the fingers."

The author concludes that the members of a consumer society are themselves consumer commodities, and it is the quality of being a commodity Education & Reality, for them, that establishes their value in the labor market.

In this context, the concepts of responsibility and responsible choice, which previously resided in the realm of ethical duty and moral concern for the other, have been transferred or taken into the realm of self-realization.

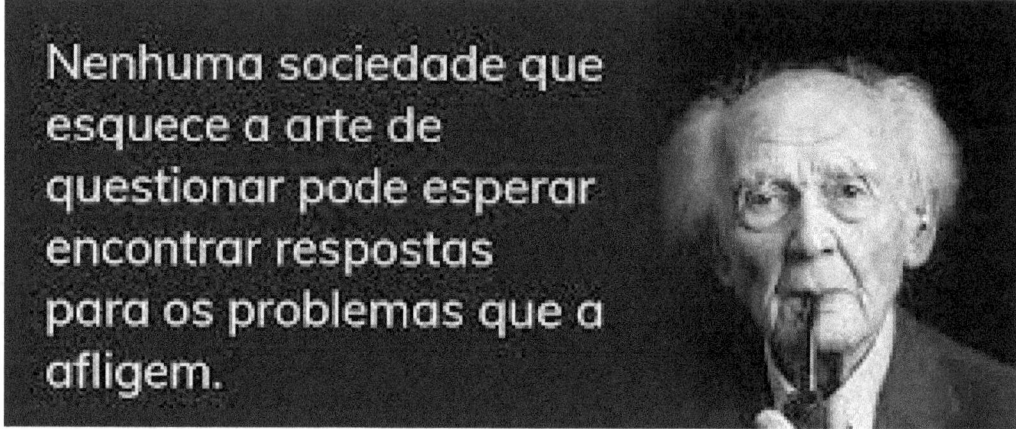

Figure 6 Bauman and his family.

In order to be recognized by others, by their tribe, subjects must be part of this logic of consumption, at the risk of being ridiculed and considered less capable than others.

From this same perspective, schooling and learning become a commodity like so many others. Knowledge is valued in its instrumental dimension to meet this consumer demand. Bauman does not deal with schooling in his analysis of the consumer society, but he explains that neither learning nor forgetting can escape the impact of the tyranny of the moment, aided and abetted by the continuous state of emergency and time dissipated into a series of heterogeneous and apparently only apparently disconnected new beginnings.

The life of consumption can be nothing other than a life of rapid learning, but it must also be a life of rapid forgetting. Forgetting is just as important as learning – if not more.

The author states that the dominant conception of learning in this society does not escape the tyranny of the moment; It is necessary to be quick to respond to this state of emergency.

From this perspective, schooling is valued, in large part, because it enables the diploma, materialized as a consumer commodity, as a necessary passport to a better future.

As a consequence, employability and the value of human capital are as ephemeral as social media posts. If knowledge is forgettable, the value of experience follows the same path.

The diploma largely justifies the investment in studies, but in recent decades, this justification has been increasingly contradictory, since the relationship between society and school education has been transformed.

If in the past few had access to the highest levels of study and, therefore, the diploma in a way guaranteed a place in the job market, today, although the diploma is valued in this society, it is not guaranteed that obtaining it will be the passport to a better future, as in the past.

The current discourse of consumerism in relation to learning is permeated by the prerogative of access to the new, to the most up-to-date learning. Bauman also explains that, like so many other commodities for consumption, learning is also understood in this logic of forgetting, because it will be necessary to renew it, always, in the search to learn something new; Therefore, we can infer that, in this logic,

"Learning should be something quick, disposable."

It would not take the effort, the dedication of time of intellectual work to obtain such learning.

In this sense, Gauchet's arguments dialogue with those presented by Bauman. Gauchet focuses in his arguments that the crisis of meaning that the school transmits in our society can be explained, among other aspects, by the loss of the dimension of tradition and by the alteration of the social status of knowledge, knowledge and culture.

For the author, in recent decades we have undergone an emptying of the value of the past, a change in the way we relate to it; in other words, for a change in the status of knowledge.

According to Gauchet, this process involves making the past a patrimony, something collectively venerated but external to our lives. We visit it, but we don't feel the need to appropriate it out of a belief that it's possible to live without it. The subject assists, therefore, the objectification of knowledge, a work attributed to experts.

Figure 7 – Marcel Gouchet.[2]

The information arrives without other mediation, we don't have to work to receive it and we receive it passively, such as information from television, the

---

[2] French philosopher and historian born in 1946 in Poilley. Director of studies emeritus at the École des Hautes Etudes en Sciences Sociales. He was editor-in-chief of the magazine Le Débat (Gallimard), one of the leading French intellectual journals, which he founded with Pierre Nora in 1980 and which he died in 2020.

Internet, etc. New technologies are considered to be able to quickly deliver the new information we so desperately need.

We're eager to get them.

For Gauchet, these transformations affect the status of knowledge and culture in our society. The meaning of knowledge is sought on an individual scale. There is a devaluation of knowledge of the past, as if it had nothing to tell us.

Previously, the references of who we are were built through our inscription in the past and in the group of which we were a part, and, currently, it is privileged to work on the knowledge of the present and anticipate the future.

In the context of education, a fundamental question arises about the content to be taught: what should be selected from the vast and diverse culture to compose the basis of teaching? This dilemma reveals an automatic non-legitimization of the culture transmitted by previous generations, implying a critical reflection on the values and knowledge that are being passed on.

At the same time, there is an intrinsic appreciation of the act of learning, often understood as a natural and spontaneous process, and a conscious and diligent effort is dispensable to achieve it. This conception, in turn, promotes the construction of another representation of knowledge and learning in the individual's life, shaping their worldview and establishing the foundations of their intellectual and cultural formation.

According to Gauchet, society renounces its function of intellectualization. Bauman explains that, in this consumer society, in addition to the excess of goods to consume, there is also a large amount of information available to serve this logic of search for the new, of meeting the demands of the present time.

Jair Santos, in turn, analyzes the invasion of mass and individual electronic technology that has occurred since the 1980s of the last century in our society, a process that became known as the Computer Age. Technology has become a mediator of the relationship between subjects and the world, by increasingly programming their daily lives and remaking this world as a spectacle.

The economy has moved into a phase of personalized consumption, and in this way it tries to seduce the individual in isolation and in his hedonistic morality. For this author, these and other transformations are typical of post-industrial societies, based on Information. Machado (2004) criticizes the way subjects in our society relate to this avalanche of information.

He explains that this society is sometimes referred to as the knowledge society and sometimes as the information society. It emphasizes that access to information does not necessarily mean having an ascent to knowledge or, in other words, to the possibility for the subject to reflect on the world, to expand their relationship with knowledge (Charlot, 2000), that is, their ways of understanding the world, others and themselves.

1.1 The difficult relationship between school students and their version as professionals.

One cannot deny the confrontation between the secular model of the school institution, which is still strong today, and these changes in the relationship of subjects with learning in our society.

The roots of the school form are based on the transmission of a truth, from a unique perspective that should be reproduced to the subjects in order to enter the world of legitimate Culture.

From this same perspective, if the ways of learning at school still show signs of these roots of the modern school form, the tensions in the school space in relation to how to relate to new technologies are also evident, among other aspects, because it becomes difficult for those who adhere to a certain way of conceiving what it is to learn at school. consider the processes of learning from other cultural artifacts legitimate, as Costa explains.

This space of tensions is intensified in school institutions, which, involved with these issues, are also confronted with other challenges. These institutions are the result of the massification of education and receive young people and adults who in the past did not have access to schooling.

They arrive at this high school and envision getting the diplomas for a better future. Therefore, the idea of obtaining a diploma as an external reason for being in high school is articulated with the dominant view of learning as a commodity of rapid consumption, a view that in turn becomes strengthened by the dominant school form itself, of transmitting knowledge as truths to provide learning in school.

Figure 8 – Is learning really useful?

There are several challenges. Despite the government's discourses of democratization of access to studies, advances in the feasibility of quality in basic education and in the expansion of access to secondary education.

One cannot deny the important place of television and the internet, for example, as enablers of varied information and the potential of the virtual world to provide new ways of socializing, relating to others, and contacting the world. However, it is necessary to mediate, problematize and denaturalize the information conveyed as truths.

The critical use of technologies can not only allow the student to have access to varied and up-to-date information, but also offer conditions for a different study practice and knowledge, opening space for curiosity and creativity and new possibilities of information and discovery; expansion of its universe of reference and exchange with other cultures.

Learning at school can play a privileged role in this sense, and the challenges of the social quality of basic education and, in particular, of secondary education cannot be addressed if there is no deepening of the complaints of young people and adults themselves in relation to the difficulties in appropriating school learning.

However, thinking about the issue of learning involves other aspects, among them, that the objective conditions are ensured and that the teachers involved in it can participate as actors in the ways of thinking about the challenges of teaching in this context.

> *One does not learn to think critically if there are no spaces for authorship, for creation for those who are mediators and participants in this process.*

As Biarnès explains, working with the diversity of students in the school, both from a cultural point of view and from their singularities, cannot be interpreted as simply the act of seeking to know the cultural and individual reality of each student.

To know a priori about the other is to close the possibility of this emergency.

These questions are fundamental when it is intended to enable spaces in high school for the denaturalization of the dominant ways of learning as a commodity and as a mere reception of ready-made truths, which presupposes considering legitimate the circulation of contemporary cultural artifacts as learning objects, such as information obtained by the media, the internet, social networks, as long as they are problematized. questioned, investigated.

Technologies in themselves are neither a problem nor a lifeline for school education. The discussions and proposals for the use of these cultural artifacts in high school and in any space of school education need to be inserted in the processes of political struggle against certain representations about the ways of learning, so that all students, and especially those who have recently been able to enter it, have access to significant processes of appropriation of knowledge and, Therefore, there should be advances in the feasibility of the propagated social quality of basic education.

The question remains:

How to train professionals who bring their human capital with them when schools are so empty of content?

1.2 THE INFORMATION CHALLENGE

Most authors, when addressing the topic of information, begin their thinking by arguing that humanity has always been linked to a variety of data and that the ubiquity of the Internet materializes an increasingly complex informational landscape.

That's that! Here it could not be different, because this context is the reason for the studies, and guidelines and conclusions that I bring to you in this book.

The exponential evolution of the volume of information made available by databases in the information systems that feed applications and portals makes it necessary to develop efficient methods of analysis and organization of large amounts of information.

This challenge gave rise to Information Science.

Information science, according to Wikipedia, is an interdisciplinary field primarily concerned with the analysis, collection, classification, manipulation, storage, retrieval, and dissemination of information. In other words, this science studies information from its genesis to the process of transforming data into knowledge.

Some professionals claim that Information Science can be divided into six theoretical currents. They are:

1. Studies of a mathematical nature (including information retrieval and bibliometrics).

2. Systems theory (origin in principles of biology).

3. Critical theory (these are mainly grounded in the humanities – particularly philosophy and history).

4. Theories of classification and representation.

5. Studies in scientific production and communication.

6. User studies (its objective was to map characteristics of a given population in order to plan the most appropriate information to be offered for education and socialization purposes).
7. Among the areas of study of this science I consider that the main ones are data modeling, dictionary and control of historical data.

The professional who studies and works with Information Science has as his field of action all areas of knowledge of the human being, such as cinematheques, data centers, libraries. Hospitals, cultural centers, public administration organizations, and private organizations from all sectors, as they all need to organize, store, and retrieve their information in the best possible way and as quickly as technology allows.

However, information science is not the result of today's technological evolution. In the last century, the first and second world wars had already transformed the informational scenario of societies into an extremely fertile scenario for the management of data produced by everyone in all jobs.

Appointed as head of the National Research Committee, later known as the Office for Scientific Research and Development, by U.S. President Franklin Roosevelt, he had the mission of coordinating the work of more than 6,000

American and European scientists. This group of scientists had their work and efforts directed them to the confrontation of World War II.

Figure 9 - Vannevar Bush.

At the end of World War II, he defined the structure of the American research system, presented in a report submitted to the then President Truman under the name of "*Science, the endless frontier*", Bush (1945).

Figure 10– Science, the endless frontier.

This report had a huge impact when it was published and continues to affect scientific activity in many countries, including Brazil.

The great impact of this report was underpinned by the reputation of Bush, who during the previous years had headed the Office of Scientific Research and Development attached to the U.S. Presidency and overseen major U.S. scientific projects in World War II, including the development of radar and the atomic bomb.

This scenario is really important, but I rescued Bush's performance to recover another article written by him: *As we may think*, Bush (1945).

Figure 11 – As we may think.

In this article he analyzes the possibilities for the future of science and technology in times of peace. Among the challenges, he deals with the recording and transmission of information and speculates on how it would be possible for scientists to read and understand so many articles and reports and from this universe to pinpoint what is really relevant. Notice that in these times the usual medium was paper, pencils, and binders.

The main challenges listed by Bush mainly dealt with:

- The difficulty of training adequate human resources in the short term.

- The storage and retrieval material used in the archives.

- The theoretical-methodological framework in use in the organization, storage and retrieval of information generated during the war.
- *As We May Think* was first cited, in a letter to the editor of Fortune magazine in 1939, its full publication published in the Atlantic Monthly and the focus of observations and comments in Life magazine.

It is common ground that Information Science was founded in 1945 with the publication of *As we may think*, having as its main merit the paradigm shift in science and technology, considering in its framework the professionals, the work instruments and the stage of the practices of representation and retrieval of information.

Bush introduced the idea that it was necessary to associate words and concepts in the indexing of information, having as its central justification the thesis that this would be the pattern that the human brain uses to associate information and transform it into knowledge.

From this idea it was possible to conclude, undeniably, that the classification and indexing systems existing at the time were limited and non-intuitive. According to Bush, storage processes should retrieve information through processes elaborated from the association of concepts, in line with the title of the article: how we think.

The year 1958 is recognized as one of the milestones in the formalization of the new discipline, as it was the year in which the Institute of Information Scientists (IIS) was founded in the United Kingdom.

The use of the term information scientist may have been introduced with the intention of differentiating these professionals from laboratory scientists, since the main interest of the former was the organization of scientific and technological information.

Figure 12 – Einstein and the questioning.

It took another 45 years for a significant fact to emerge in the world of information processing. In 1989, Tim Berners-Lee (Figure 13), an English physicist working at the Swiss laboratory CERN, brought Bush's proposal to life. He created the HTML programming language, *Hyper Text Mark up Language*, and hyperlinks widely used on the Internet.

Information science is now related to other sciences, such as archival science, administration, systems analysis, library science, computer science, social communication, accounting, information architecture, production engineering, software engineering, knowledge management, information management, project management, history, memory, and museology.

Figure 13 - Tim Berners-Lee.

Currently, the professional with a degree in one of the segments of Information Science, better known as an information professional or "information manager" professionally performs the functions of:

1. Data Administrator;

2. Information Analyst;

3. Information Scientist;

4. Information Consultant;

5. Information manager or content manager, namely on the Internet;

6. Information resources manager;

7. Information systems manager.
8. Broadening our vision to the current scenario of information processing and transmission technology, we have an expanded concept of this segment of science: information technology – the so-called IT.

Information technology was initially understood as the use of scientific knowledge or other type of organized knowledge to process information and enable human decision-making processes.

The search for information and knowledge arises from the need to sustain work processes and leads us to deal with technologies in which their users search, with a greater or lesser degree of complexity, which directly influences the volume of information retrieved. Currently we have a production of information comparable to the mass production of automobiles on their assembly line.

Figure 14 - Information or mess?

The massification of information, both in its production and in its transmission and use, has expanded the meaning of Information Technology to everything that concerns or involves the storage, processing, security, production and access to information by electronic means, that is, it is present in practically all areas today.

The world of information is a universe in its own right, and it expands faster every day. With the advent of the Internet the volume of downloads, uploads, post, search, messages sent and received, videos watched every minute is enormous. The following Figure shows the overall growth in production.

According to data compiled by Lori Lewis of the website lorilewismedia.com, 60 seconds on the web in 2021 comprise the numbers shown in Figure 16.

The IT professional's professional training area covers a number of professions and is not limited to a single training. The area involves a series of professions, which can be learned in undergraduate, graduate or technological courses, depending on the desired position.

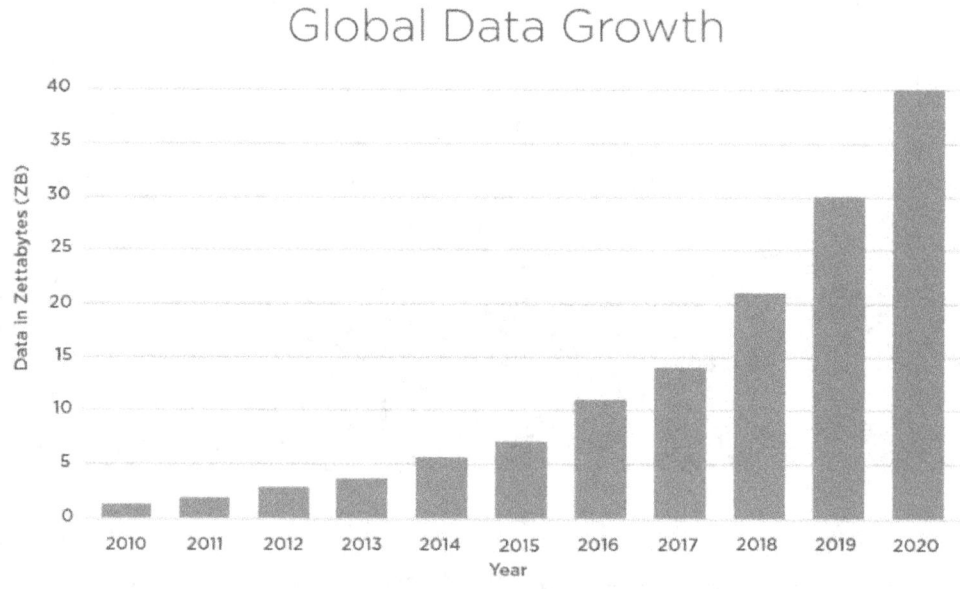

Figure 15 – Growth in data production

And speaking of profession, this professional needs to have basic skills, such as analytical vision, knowledge of methodologies, spatial vision, deduction skills, knowledge of various areas of knowledge, vocabulary, team management skills, clear and efficient communication, flexibility of thought and attitudes, responsibility, data management, project management, patience, being up to date. The following Figure expands on this list.

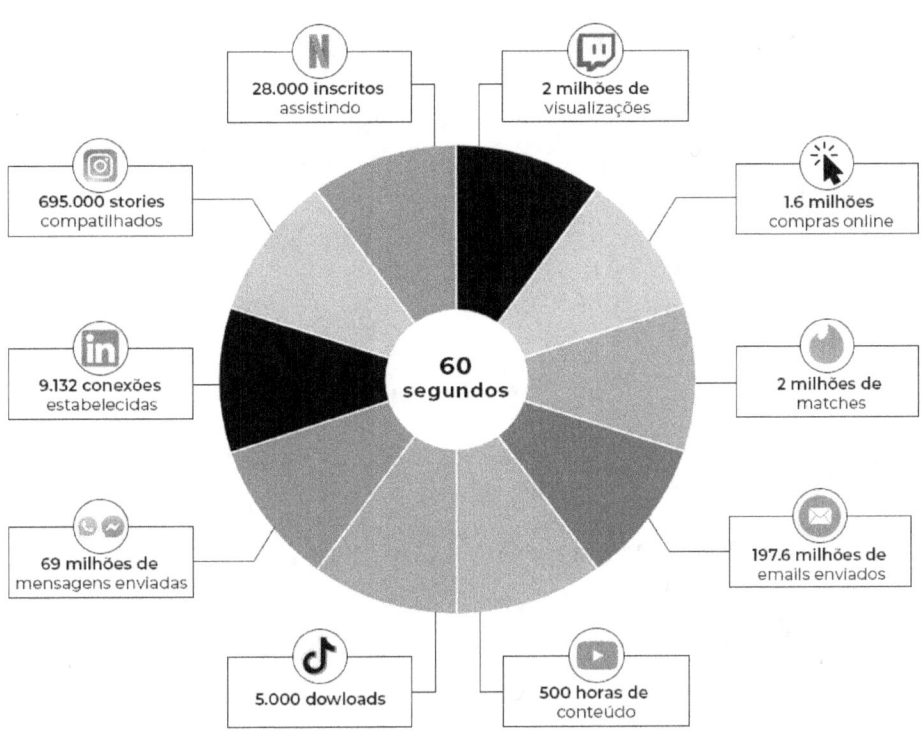

Figure 16 – One minute on the Internet in 2021.

Among the professions that stand out the most in this segment, we can mention:

- Data Administrator (AD).

- Database Administrator (DBA).

- Social Media Analyst.

- Information Security Analyst.

- Systems Analyst.

- Information Architect.

- Computer network architect.

- Data Scientist.

- IT Consultant.

- Developer.

- Data Engineer.

- Software Engineer.

- IT Governance Manager.

- Information Technology Manager.

- Marketing Digital.

- Programmer.

Figure 17 – Skills of the IT professional.

2 INFORMATION – THE RAW MATERIAL OF EVERYTHING.

> *"The best use that can be made of your data...*
> *it will certainly be developed by others and not by you."*
> Tim Berners-Lee

As pointed out by different authors, in the most different approaches, INFORMATION is a term that has had its proliferation greatly expanded since the 30's. Currently it incorporates in its meaning terms such as: post, tweet, comment, message, news, news, news, data, knowledge, quote, symbol, sign, tip, orientation and suggestion.

Figure 18 - Is a magnifying glass useful?

Our current dependence on information is so vast that it can be addressed in the famous phrase of Carl Sagan (1977):

> *"Information and food are the necessary conditions for the survival of the human being."*

It is undeniable that information is indispensable for any and all human activities. And its importance has grown so much that it has given rise to expressions such as the information industry, the information society, the information explosion, the information age, the information revolution and, the most radical of all, the post-information society society.

Information is an element of research in the most diverse areas, and its scope goes beyond the human limit and social organizations and is configured in a philosophical category related to matter, space, movement, time and energy.

Dealing with origins, the word information comes from the Latin *informare* which means:

- Modeler, narrow shape.
- Putting into the shape or appearance of something.
- To create, to represent, to present, an idea or notion something that is put into form, in order.

Breton and Proulx (1989) deal with the etymology of the word information and take up a much broader universe of meaning: a threatened society places sculptures, animated statues, giants, whose function would be to intervene in situations in which man had failed. The reference to these statues is found beyond Greco-Roman antiquity, in the creation of Rabbi Loew: the Golem of Prague.

The Golem was created in the year 1580 in Prague by Rabbi Yehuda Loew, known as the Maharal of Prague. Joseph, or Golem, was created from the four elements (fire, earth, water, and air) through the Kabbalistic knowledge of the Maharal who obtained Divine permission to draw on special spiritual forces to create a being like the Golem.

Let's take a break from technical truths and look at the Golem, figuratively, as a man-made resource with superhuman powers, as a replacement for increasingly powerful information systems. He was a holly, lifeless being, and he walked and obeyed all the Maharal's commands.

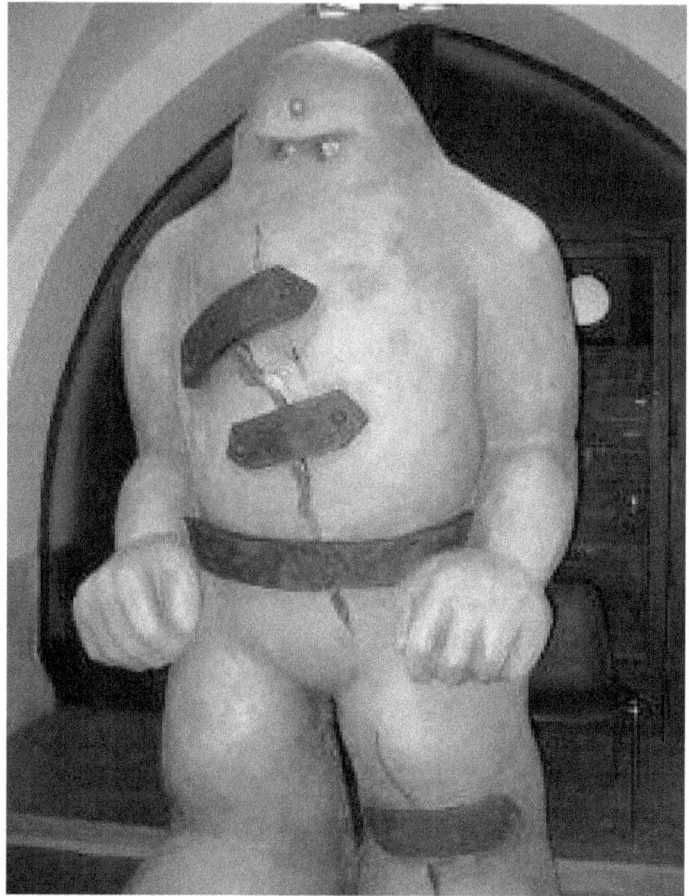

Figure 19 – The Prague Golem.

The Golem, in legend, was created with the aim of protecting Jews who were threatened with extermination through the intrigue of their enemies and saved them by sparing many lives.

The same applies to our systems and applications that promise to elevate human life to levels of quality and benefit never dreamed of. But let's move on to the legend.

The Golem was activated, brought to life, by the rabbi placing in its mouth a piece of parchment made by a magic spell in the name of the God of the Jews. The scroll was named after shem. The rabbi gave the orders to the Golem and he carried them out *ipsis literis*. Being an indestructible and extremely strong creature, he turned the nightmare of extermination into salvation.

Figure 20 – The Golem and the Rabbi.

When the Jewish people were no longer threatened, their existence lost their meaning, but the rabbi continued to use the Golem for tasks that did not require active thought. He swept the floors, fetched water, and cut wood, among countless other fatiguing orders.

The giant was a formidable workforce and didn't need to eat, drink, or rest. When Friday came, the rabbi would remove the *shem* from his mouth and the Golem would stand as static as a mannequin until the end of the Jewish Sabbath, which is the holy day of rest for the Jewish people. After that day, his master would put the paper back into his mouth, so that he would come back to life.

But there was a Sabbath when the rabbi, who was busy preparing a ceremony in the synagogue, forgot to remove the *shem* from the Golem's mouth. As he had been ordered to clean the house by a command that did not say when to finish cleaning, he began to extrapolate the cleanliness of furniture and objects, even breaking them. The debris was considered as dirt by the Golem and its cleaning generated new debris.

As the Sabbath ceremony began in the temple, the rabbi was warned that something terrible was happening in his home. When asked what was going on, the frightened citizens told him that the Golem was destroying everything in its path.

The rabbi went to the house and when he found the Golem destroying everything, he plucked up the courage and approached him telling him the command to end the cleanup. The Golem looked at the rabbi and shuddered, becoming immobilized, that's when the rabbi removed the *shem* from his mouth. Then the Golem fell like a clay doll.

Although it is a legend that deals with the will of the human being to be a creator God and to have several "moral lessons", it serves to discuss the issues addressed by Breton and Proulx (1989) and other authors who deal with the information society and the word information in the sense of creating something in the form of an idea.

This sense, one of the noblest that is given to information, brings to us creators of technology the responsibility for creating something super-powerful capable of destroying us following our orders.

In the Marvel Studios movie Age of Ultron, we have a retelling of this legend in which Tony Starck creates a computer program, an artificial intelligence, which aimed to preserve world peace, called Ultron.

Complications and script liberties aside, Ultron decides to exterminate the human race for being the cause of the problems on Earth. Hence the Avengers had to band together to destroy their own creature.

Figure 21 – Ultron, a villain product of information.

Figure 22 - Tony Stark and his technological creations.

Another retelling that is more dear to us is Mickey, Walt Disney's character, as the Sorcerer's Apprentice enchanting the brooms to fill the well with water in a moment of omnipotence.

Figure 23 - Sorcerer's Apprentice Mickey.

Notice then that we have several examples of the power of INFORM. Either as content that conveys an idea or as an action of giving shape to something. And also realize our responsibility as responsible creators of the algorithms that, ultimately, define what the creature will think, do, build.

Informatio, a variation of the verb *informare,* is the mixture of families of meanings related to knowledge and meanings that are organized around the idea of fabrication, of construction. "To put in shape", "to inform" lead to the creative image of the sculptor of the statue.

It is also worth noting the importance of the symmetrically antinomic meaning of information-construction: the inform, the formless, the monstrous. The statue, an artificial creature masterfully created by Daedalus, which gave rise to the Delic style, allowed the human being to create the formless.

See the burden of suffering sculpted in *Laocoön and His Sons*, by the artists of the island of Rhodes: Agesander, Athenodoros and Polyclitus.

Thus, according to him, information is the classification of something: symbols and their links in a relation. This relationship can be the organization of organs and functions of living beings, of a social system, or of a community. And it is also a philosophical term, because of its capacity to generate material reality and its capacity to generate organization, to classify into a system.

Information is, along with time, space, and motion, another fundamental form of matter's existence. It is the quality of evolution, the ability to reach higher stages. It is not a principle that could exist beyond matter and independently of it, but impregnated, even inseparable from it.

Matter could not exist without organization, just as it could not exist without the passage of time, and motion could not be perceived without space.

INFORMATION is, in fact, a term full of meanings. A series of concepts interconnected by sophisticated relationships and not a single and simple concept.

Defining what information is requires an analysis of the spectrum of definitions in which information can be inserted. For Yuexiao (1988), the philosophical spectrum is immersed in a context in which the sources, nature and function of information are discussed.

Figure 24 - Laocoön and His Sons.

The opinions of philosophers may not converge, but it is common ground that information is not a specific type of object, nor does it have any specific content. For them, it is a vehicle for interrelationships and interactions between objects and contents.

In another context, Zeman (1970) argues that information is the organization of elements or parts, material or not, in some way, in some classified system.

Araújo (1991) states that information suffers from the gigantism caused by the vast literature it has been generating. According to her, there are more than 400 concepts, definitions and approaches used by the academic world.

Belkin's review of information concepts highlights the importance of the different points of view of authors such as Goffmann, Yovits, Otten, Artandi, Brooks, Mikhailov, Chernyi and Giliarevskii, Barnes, Fairthorne, Gindin, Wersig, Robertson, Shannon, Lynch, Nauta, Belzer, Shreider and Pratt, among others.

The authors searched for the basic idea of the term information and found that the only basic notion common to all uses of information is the idea of structures being changed, thus leading to the concept that information is what is capable of transforming structures.

> "Thus, from the concept of structure, specifically, the structure of the image that an organism has of itself and of the world, an information context is constructed with a typology of increasing complexity in which information, in its broadest sense, is that which changes or transforms such structure. In this context, information only occurs within organisms – from the hereditary level to that of formalized knowledge" (Araújo, 1995).

Take the case of semiotic structures such as texts, maps, and scores, which are contents that will only be information by modifying the cognitive structure of a living organism. These contents are data and are expressed in languages, images, musical notes, numeric or alphanumeric characters and electronic impulses, which, when transmitted by some means of communication, may or may not generate information.

Setzer (1986), in his analysis of databases, states that a datum can be defined as a sequence of quantified or quantifiable symbols and concludes:

> *"Therefore, a text is a given. In fact, letters are quantified symbols, since the alphabet itself constitutes a numerical base. Images, sounds, and animation are also given, as they can all be quantified to the point that someone who comes into contact with them may have difficulty distinguishing their reproduction, from the quantified representation, with the original."*

We have, then, that Information is something complex and is in essence an extremely polysemic term and, allied to knowledge, it was adopted as a *delimiting locus*, reaching all sectors of society and areas of knowledge. This adoption only increased the ambiguities of the term, given the different views and conceptualizations that began to refer to it.

2.1 History of Little Red Riding Hood in the headlines of major magazines and newspapers

The fable of Little Red Riding Hood, Charles Perrault, is an excellent example of how complex it is to transmit information content through a set of different origins to different destinations.

Let's go to the scenarios in the media.

JORNAL NACIONAL: (William Bonner): "Good evening. A 7-year-old girl was devoured by a wolf last night." (Renata Vasconcellos) "But thanks to the work of a hunter, there wasn't a tragedy."

FANTÁSTICO (Poliana Abritta): "... How cute, guys, you won't believe it, but this beautiful girl here was pulled alive from the belly of a wolf, isn't it...

CITY WARNS: "... Where are we going to end up, where are the authorities? Where are the authorities? The girl was walking to her grandmother's house. There's no public transportation! There's no public transportation! And it was devoured alive. A wolf, a naughty wolf. Put it on the screen, cousin! Because I really say, I'm not afraid of the wolf, I'm not afraid of the wolf!

Figure 25 - The Wolf and Little Red Riding Hood.

O Estado de S. Paulo: Greenpeace denounces the killing of wolves and warns: this wolf is an endangered species.

FOLHA DE S. PAULO: Photo caption: "Little Red Riding Hood, on the right, shakes hands with her savior." In the article, a box with a zoologist explaining the eating habits of wolves and a huge infographic showing how Little Red Riding Hood was devoured and then saved by the woodcutter.

ISTOÉ: Recordings reveal that Lobo was an advisor to an influential politician.

SEE:... So-and-so, 23, the woodcutter who pulled Little Red Riding Hood out of the wolf's belly has been hailed as a hero in the region. "The wolf was sleeping, I don't think it was that dangerous," he admits.

HUMAN CAPITAL AT WORK

JORNAL DO BRASIL: "Forest: Girl is attacked by wolf". (In the article, we don't know where, or when, or more details.)

THE GLOBE: "Living Removal from the Belly of a Wolf". (In the article, there will even be a map of the region. The save is more important than the attack.)

POPULAR NEWS: Blood and tragedy at Grandma's house.

CLAUDIA Magazine: How to get to grandma's house without being fooled by the wolves on the way.

NOVA Magazine: Ten ways to drive a wolf crazy in bed.

MARIE-CLAIRE: In bed with a wolf and my grandmother, an account of someone who went through this experience.

CARAS (with photo essay): "In the hot tub at grandma's hut, in Campos de Jordão, Little Red Riding Hood reflects on the events: "until I was devoured, I didn't value many things in life, today I'm a different person" she admits.

WHIM: That Wolf is a Cat!

PLAYBOY (Photo essay with Little Red Riding Hood in the month of the scandal): Cover title: "See what only the wolf saw".

SEXY (Photo essay with Little Red Riding Hood a year after the scandal): Cover headline: "That girl killed a wolf!"

G MAGAZINE (photo essay with lumberjack): Cover title: "Lumberjack shows the axe."

That's that! Conceptualizing INFORMATION is not a trivial task. In the above accounts, all versions are true and all convey a part of the original informational content. But none of them were exempt or complete.

And since we know that a multitude of errors in the conception and transmission of information is possible, it may be that there was not even a wolf in the reported event.

2.2 The value of information

Several authors are dedicated to discussing and elucidating the value of information as a source for strategic lines of action, work plans, planning of future scenarios and changes in the market of public or private organizations.

Among them, it is possible to cite Helbig et al. (2012) who deal in particular with the initial motivation indispensable to arouse society's interest in this information and Barreto (1996) who considers that the value of information depends directly on the personal skills of the consumer, the educational level of society and the workforce as a whole.

The demand for information in Brazil can be seen in the model proposed by Barreto (1996), Figure 10, in which it is classified as:

A. Demand for information: configures a demand oriented to reflection, for the re-elaboration of the information received, the information to sustain and support science and technology. It is the segment of the information market with the greatest scarcity, but it is the one that concentrates the greatest effort in preparing and distributing the information supply.
B. Maintaining Demand: which can be understood as the information responsible for maintaining the individual in his/her professional and social status quo.
C. Utilitarian Demand: the demand for information for the current transactions of the individual when exercising his citizenship. It can be seen that nowadays the supply of information is small and does not cover the potential demand.

Analyzing the case of information production in the public sector, Table 1 presents the relationship between some types and the main demands and applications in various segments of society (Ávila, 2015).

Government institutions are identified as big data creators in various segments, such as health, financial, tourism, geographic, and security information.

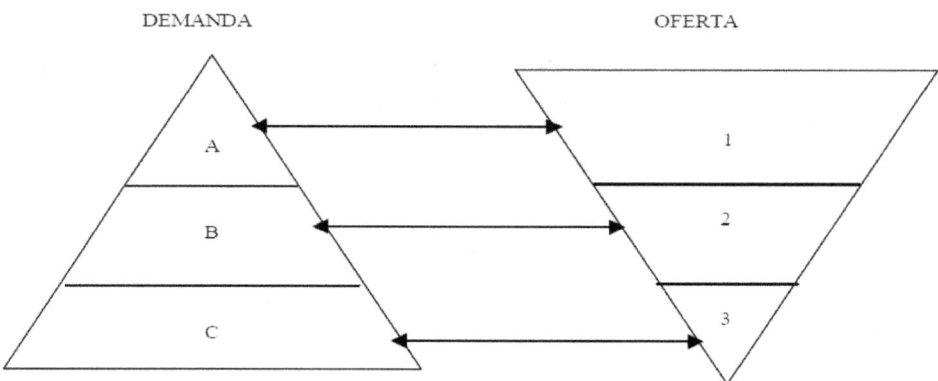

Figure 26 – Model of the relationship between supply and demand.

In this context of demand and supply market, with the Internet and open data as *the locus*, in agreement with Manyika (2011) and Ubaldi (2012), information can be classified into 4 categories, as shown in Figure 11, based on open government data:

- Big Data. Databases that go beyond the limits of the processing capacity of the information systems available today. The volume of data is on the order of peta bytes.
- Open data. Data that is available to the citizen, without cost or restrictions of any kind coming from any source, whether private or public.
- Open government data: This is what government institutions make available to citizens.
- Personal data: These are personal data of each person, such as income tax, address, consumption.

Segmento	Tipo de Informação Pública	Finalidade
Setor Produtivo	Indicadores Sociais, Econômicos, Demográficos, Planos de Governo, Relatórios Fiscais, Informações Geográficas (imagens aéreas, vetores com distâncias entre localidades, mapas e cartogramas sobre dados socioeconômicos), etc.	Projetos de Consultoria; Expansão e/ou Manutenção de Negócios; Desenvolvimento ou aprimoramento de produtos e serviços
Setor Acadêmico	Indicadores Sociais, Econômicos, Demográficos, Planos de Governo, Relatórios Fiscais, Informações Geográficas (imagens aéreas, vetores com distâncias entre localidades, mapas e cartogramas sobre dados socioeconômicos), etc.	Artigos Científicos; Trabalhos Acadêmicos; Projetos de Pesquisa; Monografias; Dissertações; Teses; Projetos para captação de recursos em instituições de fomento
Setor Público	Indicadores Sociais, Econômicos, Demográficos, Planos de Governo, Relatórios Fiscais, Informações Geográficas (imagens aéreas, vetores com distâncias entre localidades, mapas e cartogramas sobre dados socioeconômicos), Pesquisas acadêmicas, estudos e análises, relatórios de tendência, projeções de cenários.	Diagnósticos governamentais, diagnósticos sobre áreas ou demandas específicas (ex: problemas ambientais); Formulação de planos e programas de governo, execução de ações, monitoramento e avaliação governamental; Publicidade de ações governamentais; Projetos para captação de recursos em instituições de fomento
Imprensa	Dados orçamentários e financeiros; Pesquisas e indicadores socioeconômicos; Dados Populacionais; Relatórios de Monitoramento e Acompanhamento de Ações Governamentais	Matérias e investigações jornalísticas; Publicidade de ações governamentais; Denúncias de não-conformidades em ações governamentais
Sociedade em Geral	Dados orçamentários e financeiros; Pesquisas e indicadores socioeconômicos; Dados Populacionais	Monitoramento e Controle Social do Governo; Elaboração de Projetos para captação de recursos

Table 1 – Main demands for government information.

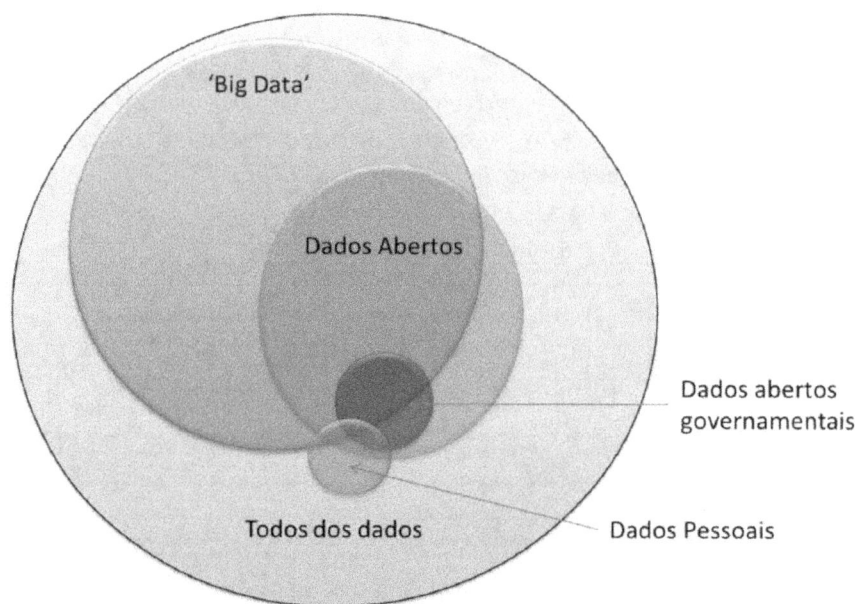

Figure 27 - Data subdivisions.

For Davies (2010), data can produce other data, information, interpretation interfaces, facts, and services. Figure 27 illustrates this chain. And notice that:

- Data produces facts when individuals looking at data sources feed the actions of organizations that generate results in the economic planning of organizations, entities, or individuals.
- Data gives rise to information that results from the cross-referencing of databases that, in turn, produce tabular information, infographics, and reports.
- Data generate interpretation interfaces by providing means of interactivity between one or more databases, such as: interactive maps, links to other data.
- Data produces other data when it is processed and originates from other data sources.

- Data generates monitoring of the quality of services when open data supports the provision of online services, such as the identification of anomalies in public services by the population and their communication to the authorities.

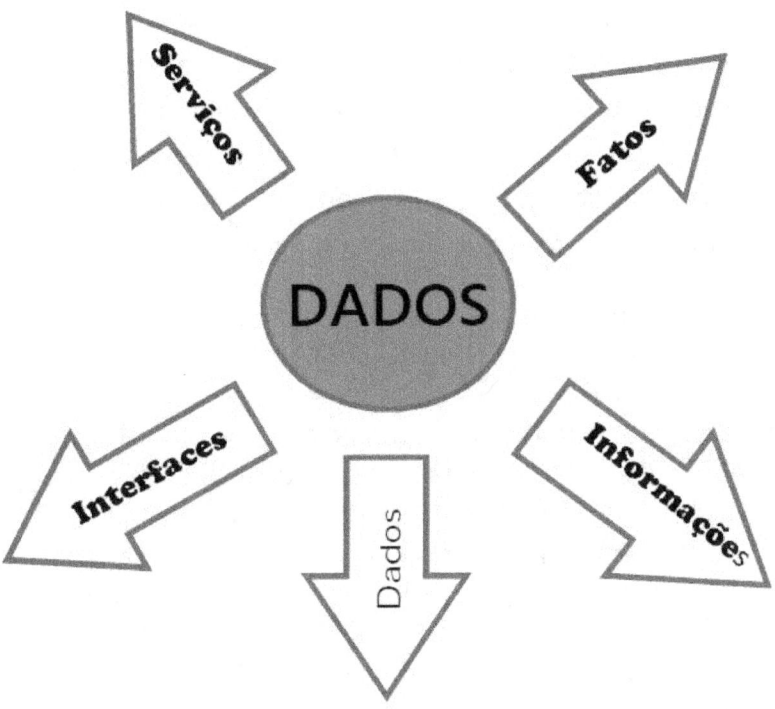

Figure 28 - What the data can produce.

However, in recent decades there has been a change in this production chain. The focus of organizations has shifted from providing features that improve the delivery of government services to focusing on the user experience, creating information needs.

The management of information and its data brings benefits to the end user, but it brings benefits, mainly, to organizations, such as:

- Continuous improvement. Data management enhances the analysis of the performance of information systems and their products, making them easier to monitor.
- Increased productivity. Considering that every organization has among its main strategic objectives to increase its productivity, having data organized, with efficient recovery, with little redundancy and losses is a crucial factor to achieve this goal.
- Expansion of the area of operation. Managed data produces more reliable databases, which in turn support better decision-making. This type of efficient information-based management enhances all projects to increase production, maintain and expand markets and face competition.

Going further, I propose that you have basic guidelines for data management in your organization. Take the following guidelines:

- Storage: the way databases are stored should prioritize the needs of users.
- Reliability: if there are doubts about the quality of the data, the information will be a source of risk for decision-making.
- Consistency: Maintaining distributed quality control among teams that interact with data throughout the production and use chain promotes security against failures and increases reliability in database consistency.
- Straight to the basics: all data produced or held by the organization should be treated as assets.
- Enterprise model: Every data structure follows standards that aim to make it possible to maintain an enterprise data model.
- Relevance: Relevant data must be available in a timely manner and to the right user.
- Teamwork: Organization data is shared and useful to all teams.

2.3 Information and strategic information system

In order to be able to discuss data modeling and other elements of this context, it is necessary to have a concept of information. Thus, considering everything that has already been presented and analyzed, I consider as information:

> *Information is the set of data that, when provided in an appropriate way and at the right time, improves the knowledge of the person who receives it, making him more qualified to develop a certain activity or make a certain decision.*

The proper use of information as a management tool for a company is an indispensable condition for the success of that company. The type of information basically depends on the management model to which it will serve.

The information in operational management, which is essentially of internal origin and aims mainly to estimate annual expenditures of costing and new investments, differs from the information necessary for strategic management in which the emphasis is on the external environment of the company.

The diagram shown in Figure 29 illustrates the difference between the context of operational and strategic information.

Thus, an organization that intends to introduce strategic management in its administration must develop specific information systems, in parallel with existing or non-existing systems, for operational management.

According to Leitão (1993), the evolutionary process of management models begins with the greatest concern of organizations in monitoring factors related to their internal environment.

The 1960s was the initial period of the 1960s.

This scenario shifts the focus of attention from production to the market, which gives rise to strategic management as a response to the concern of organizations with the external environment, presenting as a characteristic the fact that it is constantly seeking to evaluate the future trends of evolution of the external environment in order to identify opportunities and threats for the company in order to guide it in its long-term objectives and strategies.

On the other hand, strategic management proves to be an efficient tool to respond to the failures of strategic management and a means to make it more useful to organizations.

Initially, the great concern was with the diversified activities of organizations, called "strategic business units", whose strategic planning was prepared independently of the holding company, at the time of the so-called strategic business planning.

Subsequently, in view of the great duplication of efforts in the middle activities in which the businesses ended up competing with each other, corporate strategic planning began to be used. However, after some time, it was found that there was an excessive focus on the strategic planning stage, to the detriment of the complementary and parallel stages of the process.

The fact of having strategic management does not dispense with operational management, because while strategic management is linked to the concept of effectiveness, operational management is concerned with efficiency.

And we have that the fundamental difference between strategic information and operational information with respect to the internal environment is that, in operational management, the only concern in monitoring the internal environment refers to the monitoring of the company's performance in relation to the physical and budgetary goals established a priori.

Figure 29 – Organizational vs. strategic information.

In strategic management, monitoring has several distinct levels: knowing the values and beliefs of the organizational culture, diagnosing internal capabilities, monitoring their evolution, identifying the causes of strengths and weaknesses, and monitoring the performance of what was planned.

Among the characteristics of databases for use in information systems used in operational management, I highlight:

1. They typically focus on data from the internal environment, managing information related to production data, as well as information related to new investments to meet market growth.
2. Information on the external environment is incorporated only if it is related to the increase in demand and the identification of sources of financing for new investments.

3. Information about the internal environment must be structured both to allow the elaboration of the organization's management plans, as well as for their monitoring and control.

2.4 Information and Information Retrieval Systems: genera of the same species?

The discussion in the previous sections allowed us to conceptualize information as that which alters structures, that is, it only makes sense in the effective contact between a piece of data with information potential and the user.

However, the area, perhaps due to the lack of a more complete discussion about the phenomena of information and information systems, has assumed and disseminated the designations IS and SRI, thus generating a confusion between the object worked (documents, texts and messages) and the possible effect of its content on the user, that is, the information itself.

It is important to note that the designations **SI** (Information System) and **SRI** (Information Retrieval System) are not very representative. For the purposes of this book, Information Systems will be considered synonymous with Information Retrieval Systems (SRIs), that is, they are systems that, among other functions, aim to give access to the data contained in databases persisted in them.

In this context, it can be stated that information systems are those that aim to carry out communication processes.

This information, in an expanded view, materializes the set of recorded human memory. Belkin and Robertson (1976) treat this database as a "cognitive-social" collection, conceptual structures referring to collective knowledge, that is, the structures of knowledge shared by the members of a social group (manuscripts, books, periodicals, maps, films, videos, paintings, scores, etc.).

Calvin Mooers is credited with coining the term "information retrieval" in 1951, but the modern framework for information retrieval and consolidation of SRI as an entity is generally dated from the 1940s and 1950s.

This period is identified by the need to store and retrieve, quickly and accurately, the vast number of documents that had been growing exponentially since the seventeenth century and by the advent of the computer, which was seen as "the" solution to the problems of information storage and retrieval.

In this same period, Von Bertalanffy (1968) systematized the new scientific ideas that proposed an "integrated all" approach, the systemic approach.

The simultaneous emergence of the systemic view, with the emergence of the computer and the enormous growth of literary production, led to the emergence and consolidation of the entity Information Retrieval System/Information System.

The growth limit of the information system and its subsystems has already been reached; At the moment, the transition from this growth to saturation shows problems such as:

- Selection that does not select.

- Indexing that isolates and mutilates.

- Organization of files that have problems regarding their own physical integrity.

- These problems continue to grow and have repercussions:

- In the way you store the data.

- They generate imprecision and indeterminism in the analysis and negotiation of the classification of information.

- They limit search/retrieval strategies.

- They generate niches of incoherence in the information retrieved.
- In this context, we can only accept that the gigantism of information systems is proportional to the user's dissatisfaction and frustration with the response provided by these systems.

Although quality emerges from quantity, there is a point at which overgrowth leads to saturation. The attainment of a limit point beyond which there is no longer any capacity for absorption/assimilation.

In the context of information systems, this phenomenon is clear: information has grown exponentially, it has exploded. The main concern of the IS was to follow this growth, this explosion, without questioning the possible consequences that could happen.

This scenario, without risk of making mistakes, results from the lack of understanding of the information phenomenon and confusing it with the document phenomenon – simulacrum of information.

The use of information technologies, for the most part, implements expanded and accelerated replicas of the manual processes on which they are based. The blind use of technology has generated, as might be expected, the non-use or blind use of documents.

We have, then, capacities for storing, processing and transmitting data that have been extended to inconceivable numbers, infinitely superior to man's capacity for assimilation, that is, they are being taken beyond saturation.

Still in systemic terms, it is necessary to evaluate whether the objectives of the systems are being achieved and how efficiently this is done. For this to be possible, these objectives need to be expressed in measurable terms.

The treatment of documents containing potential information presupposes an analysis of their content in order to be processed and retrieved. However, systems do not yet have the means to perform this task and depend on humans for indexing.

The success of the systemic approach is based more on its rapid, unquestioned and wide adoption by various segments of the technology world than on being an effective solution to the problems that those same segments present, including information retrieval systems.

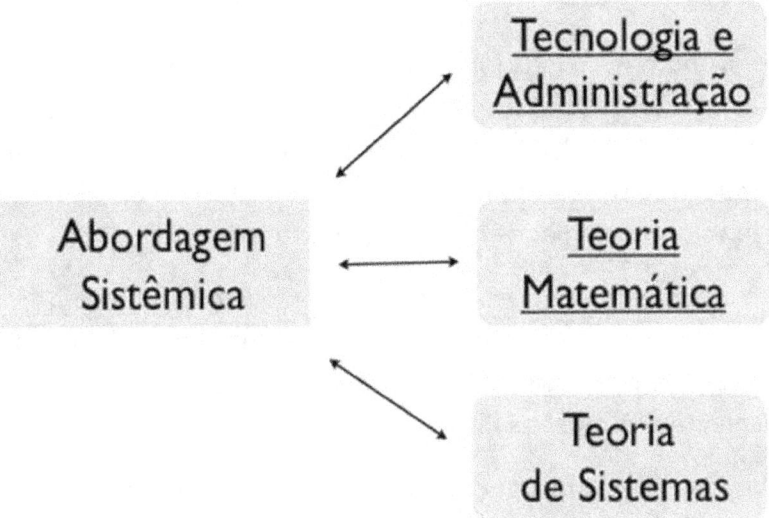

Figure 30- Systemic Approach.

Why are CRSs failing? Is it not because they need another context, another model, a new theoretical-conceptual approach that studies them as they really are and not as they imagine themselves to be?

A simple and easily verifiable example is the amount of information retrieved from an Internet search engine, be it Google, Edge or similar. You type in your search parameters and receive trillions of addresses of information as an answer.

I can say without risk of error that the user considers, at most, the first 3 pages of the retrieved information. What to do with the other recovered items? There is no point in having quantity without being able to make use of it.

You will agree with me that information, in this context, is only a probability, an uncertainty, an unpredictability, bringing it closer to the noblest paradigms of science related to chaos.

Information and Chaos, which comes first?

2.5 Chaos

The history of human evolution is marked by a search for regularity demonstrated by the order of the seasons, the precision of the movement of stars and planets in the sky, the succession of days and nights, etc. Such regularities were demonstrated by Isaac Newton more than 300 years ago, through the laws of motion and the theory of gravity.

The laws of motion explain much of our universe. According to her, natural linearity happens when the future is a direct consequence of the past, in an immaculate determinism in which chance and uncertainty are distortions that are simply neglected. Almost as if they were natural errors of the process.

But when we consider the concept of order, it carries within it its own antithesis: the existence of order implies the existence of disorder.

In the understanding of the great scientists of humanity, determinism is opposed to the idea of chance. According to Moreira (1992),

"For Newton, Galileo, Kepler, Leibniz and other scientists, determinism is linked to the idea of 'natural law,' of 'simplicity of nature,' and will find a precise expression in the mathematical formulation of physical laws."

The antithesis, almost complementarity, of determinism is chance, probability, the explanation of how a varied set of events can behave in typical ways, even though individual events are unpredictable.

The analysis of a coin's flips is an example of this behavior. It has already been determined that the probability of heads or tails is 50%, although it is impossible to predict each individual coin toss.

In the eighteenth century the French mathematician Pierre Simon da Laplace, one of the first scholars of probability and disorder, was a disciple of Newton. In the nineteenth century, Heisenberg's set of theories of the uncertainty principle shook the scientific community. Determinism and probability remained possible worldviews, despite their incompatibilities (Persival, 1992).

Quantum theory, also based on the calculus of probabilities, came in 1920-30 to challenge this situation of conflict. Chaos theory in the 1960s-70s poses a second challenge. His principle is that even in simple Newtonian systems, prediction is not always possible – there is persistent instability, that is, chaos.

In the field of concept, "chaos is disorder, it is the behavior of small changes leading to large changes later, it is persistent instability, it is unpredictability" (Yuexiao, 1988). Also according to the author, chaos seems to be the principle of information and a focus of convergence of information retrieval systems.

Chaos is a science of the computer age, of Information Science, and of communication in some of its contexts. Figure 14 illustrates this scenario.

SRIs are the result of deterministic propositions, as they are composed of input, output, limits, processing, rules, etc. Its modules run processes with defined functions.

It is necessary to incorporate the logic of chaotic reasoning to address issues such as:

1. What is the alternative that ensures the recovery and dissemination of something that can occur outside the system environment?
2. How do you know which message will actually be information for the user?
3. When it comes to selection or indexing criteria, changes, no matter how small, lead to major changes in the information retrieved.

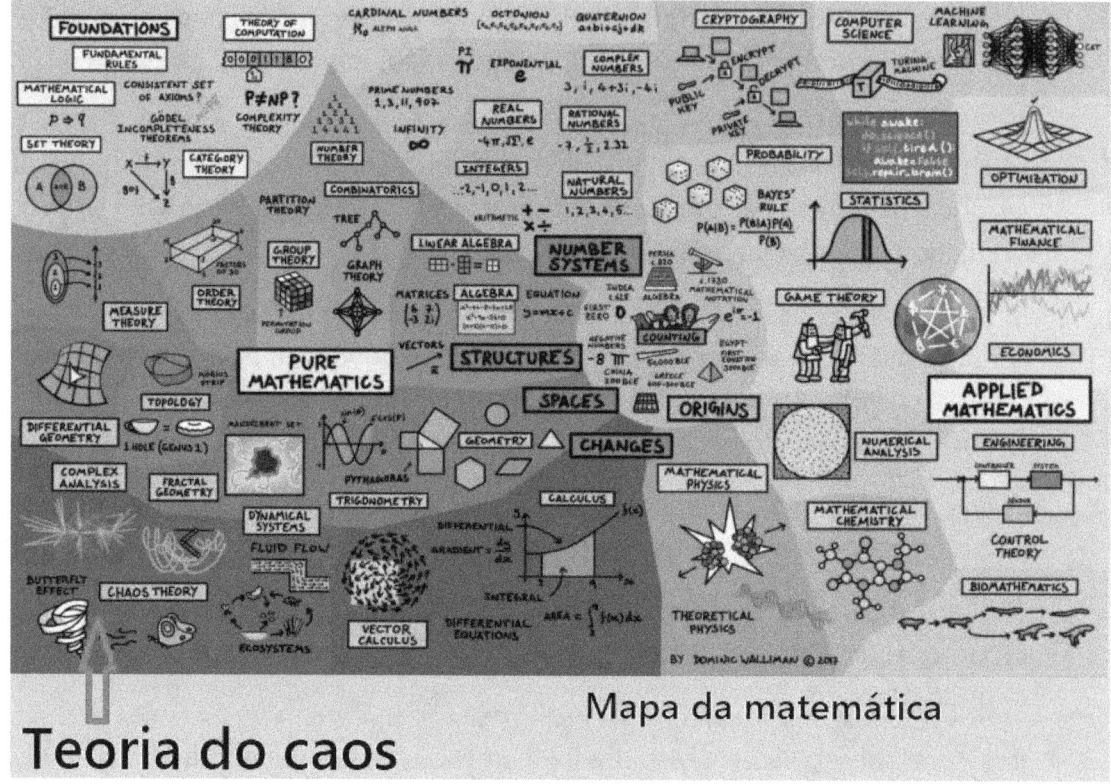

Figure 31 -Chaos.

A query handled in different ways retrieves both highly relevant and irrelevant documents.

Any change in the initial parameters of a query can affect the CRS since it has traits very similar to those of a fractal. An example of this thesis is the 80/20 law, which presents an impressive invariance in the scale. The size of the collection does not affect the result where 20% of it meets 80% of user demand. And yet, reductions in this collection to, for example, 20% of its initial size, will not significantly modify the standard, resuming the 80/20 ratio.

For many authors, complexity is the boundary between order and chaos. Thus, in complex systems there are many independent components interacting with each other in various ways. This diversity of interactions is one of the reasons for the spontaneous self-organization that occurs in such systems.

In addition, complex, self-organizing systems are also adaptive and have the ability to turn everything possible into advantages, A prime example is the human brain, organizing, reorganizing, reconfiguring billions of neuronal connections in order to learn from lived experiences.

According to Afanasiev (1977), complex systems exhibit a self-organizing and adaptive dynamism that differentiates them from static objects such as computer chips.

It should be noted that the coherence, structure and associative self-organization of complex systems are not explained only by chaos

I would like to make a provocation here. If we consider that CRS can be analyzed as complex systems, that information is something that approaches chaos and that determinism is more a special effect than a proven reality, where can we place Information Science?

Be calm, patient and follow me!

2.6 Information Science

In the 1960s and 1970s, some authors described Information Science as a science:

- Associated with the mathematical theory of communication.
- Energized by the emerging automation of CRS and databases.
- Targeted at semantic problems.
- Busy with the representation of information and with the initial studies of relevance and performance evaluation of SRIs.
- Developing work to understand the communication processes and the behavior of its users.
- Its birth formally occurred at a meeting of the Georgia Institute of Technology in 1962. It was conceptualized by Shera as:

> *"Science that investigates the properties and behavior of information, the forces that govern the flow of information, and the means of processing information for optimal accessibility and usability. Processes include the generation, dissemination, collection, organization, storage, retrieval, interpretation, and use of information. The area is derived from or related to mathematics, logic, linguistics, psychology, computer technology, operations research, graphic arts, communications, library science, management, and some other areas."*

Como parte desse nascimento o American Documentation Institute foi alterado para American Society for Information Science e seu periódico, American Documentation, teve o nome alterado para Journal of the American Society for Information Science.

As with any nascent subject area, early research in Information Science borrowed methods from other areas of science and adapted others. Its foundations were built by sets of concepts and theories, laws and quasi-laws.

Gradually, the initial questions about the contours and concerns of a science that was taking its first interthematic flights and beginning the investigation of its own object began to emerge.

Computing and automation have caused changes in processes related to information retrieval, such as cataloguing and indexing, which had to be more explicit and could then be questioned in their foundations.

However, it is logical that in order to define new paradigms, it is necessary to establish some paradigm, or at least new theoretical-conceptual contexts. Jarvelin and Vakkari (1993) stated that "The research methodology (...) received little attention."

Research in the area seems to be concentrated on the use of empirical methods, suggesting a one-dimensional treatment of theoretical assumptions and problem formulations, according to Jarvelin and Vakkari (1993) who also state:

"Methodological discussion and analysis of the fundamentals of the discipline are both prerequisites for a more diverse use of research strategies and a more comprehensive articulation of research problems. These topics should therefore receive more attention. (...) Otherwise, it is not possible to increase the conceptual clarity of existing theories."

Based on the definition of information as something that is capable of transforming structures, it is possible to question whether an Information Science is really concerned with information. And yet, what is your real object of study?

If Information Science has been dealing mainly with the organization and configuration of data packages and with the transmission of this package, isn't this an inappropriate name for this segment of knowledge?

Information Science must approach the phenomenon it intends to study: the encounter between information and the user. The power of information, combined with the modern means of mass communication, has unlimited power to culturally transform man, society and humanity itself.

In the history of humanity, there are some periods of great scientific growth, as identified by Anderla (1979), "between 1660 and 1960, all the volume indices of science multiplied by a factor of about one million".

Figure 32 – Information Science.

Nowadays there is talk of large amounts of data in the cloud, and its exponential growth began in the last century with the publication and circulation of thousands of technical journals with the results of research on the development of science and technology.

The process of bringing document and information entities closer together is a demand of today's society, oriented to diverse social segments that have different needs and particularized perceptions of information.

The SIs then move towards an inversion in their growth process to produce smaller and more adequate systems. There is no escaping the action of entropy, which makes the traditional systems view itself inadequate both in form and content, there are no open or closed systems.

IS developers need to situate themselves in Chaos and review the concepts of software engineering in the light of this theory, seeking a future more suited to a world of big data for their own theories, laws, prototypes, models, concepts, etc. As a direct consequence, there will be, at the very least, a reconceptualization in their own paradigms of creators of information and systems.

In practice, the consequences of a chaotic future are so great and of such impact that it is impossible to list them all. By way of example, we can mention a few:

- Review of the concept of what the information professional is, their training, performance and continuing education.

- Adequacy of CRS to the needs of consumers who are increasingly dependent on information.

- Deepening in a new theoretical-conceptual approach in which information is made possible by the conjunction and even by the superimposition of document entities and information systems.

- Analysis of the processing of documents as a whole, throughout their flow of availability for access, from entry to exit, transforming them into indexed information with greater potential for use.
- The situation is complex, without a shadow of a doubt, but we have the knowledge to proceed towards a world of more efficient databases that sustain a growth of information that tends to infinity.

HUMAN CAPITAL AT WORK

"Each individual is an invaluable source within an organization, and true human capital lies in the diversity of skills, knowledge, and experiences that each employee brings with them."

McKinsey & Company

3　HUMAN CAPITAL AT WORK. THE VALUE OF EXPERIENCE.

The concept of human capital has proven to be increasingly relevant in a world that is constantly changing and evolving. According to studies and analyses, human capital represents a significant part of an individual's wealth, making up two-thirds of the total on an overall average. Within this context, work experience plays a key role, contributing almost half of this value.

Work experience is not just limited to the time dedicated to a particular role or position, but encompasses the entire set of skills, competencies, and knowledge acquired throughout a person's professional career. The experience allows the worker to develop their ability to perform tasks efficiently, solve problems creatively, make sound decisions and adapt to changes and challenges in the work environment.

In addition, work experience is a determining factor in the construction of professional identity and in valuing an individual's human capital. The presence of a solid background of professional experiences can open doors, facilitate career growth and progression, and add value to a worker's resume.

It is important to emphasize that, despite the importance of work experience, the continuous search for learning and improving skills is essential for the development of human capital and for maintaining relevance in the labor market in a globalized and highly competitive scenario.

Therefore, investing in professional experience and skills development means investing in one's own growth and building a promising and successful future.

The most important resource in any economy or organization is its human capital—that is, the collective knowledge, attributes, skills, experience, and health of the workforce. Human capital development begins in early childhood and continues through formal education and spans the entire working life.

HUMAN CAPITAL AT WORK

Figure 33 – Only experience enables the professional

Human capital is much more than a macroeconomic abstraction. Each person has a unique, living, breathing ability. These capacities belong to the individual, who decides where to put them to work. The degree of choice is not unlimited, of course.

People are products of geography, family, and education; Your starting points matter. Having career options also depends on an individual's skills and attributes, their networks, their family obligations, the health of the broader labor market, and social factors. And most important of all are your soft skills.

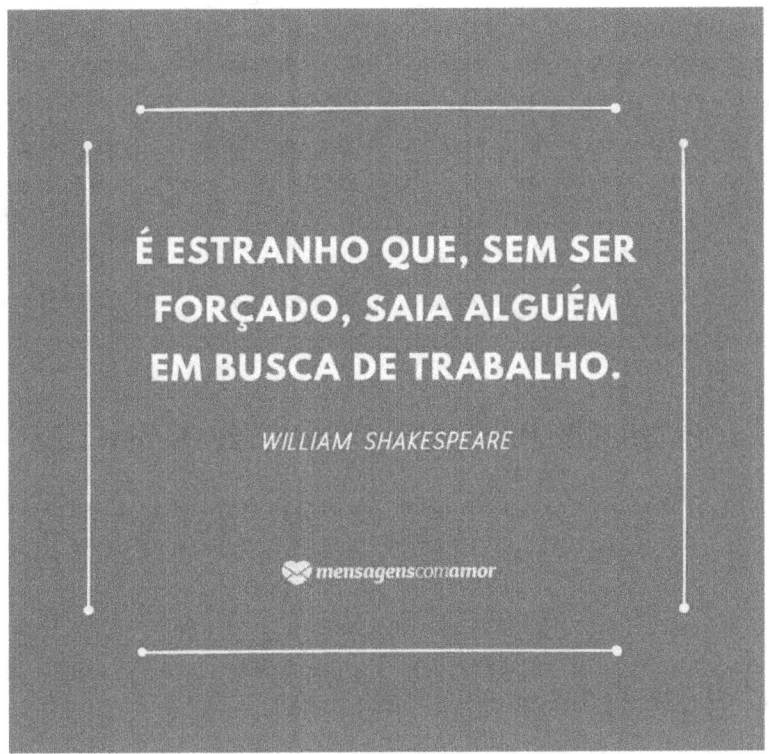

Figure 34 - Shakespeare and the search for work.

While we recognize these constraints, career moves are nonetheless an important mechanism for expanding skills and increasing earnings.

The patterns within our dataset show that switching to a new role pays off— and even more so when someone gets a new position that stretches their capabilities or represents a match that better utilizes their skills.

In a recent UN study, about one-third of workers in the U.S., Germany and the U.K., and nearly one-quarter of Indian workers, are on track to move up one or more quintiles in estimated lifetime earnings from their career starting points. This ascending mobile group stands out for making more frequent and bolder role moves.

For people without educational credentials who start in low-paying positions in particular, the move is key to increasing their earnings.

Function movements help individuals continually upgrade their skills, increase their income, and build track records that translate into value.

However, individuals can't make bold moves that represent a real leap forward unless an employer sees their potential and has a chance to hire them.

The most effective way for an individual to maximize the "experience effect" is to join an organization that prioritizes and strengthens their development.

3.1 Work experience adds to the value of human capital

The perception of the value of human capital is based on the basis of formal education and increases according to the development of the professional's soft skills.

Work experience can be defined holistically as the accumulated knowledge that workers gain from being in the workforce.

This can occur through the job itself, formal learning and development programs provided by the employer, and job changes that better match one's existing skills or allow for

Organizations structure their work environments with systems and practices that help employees become more productive. When people enter these settings, the value is created. In addition to earning wages, workers gain knowledge and new capabilities that they carry with them for the rest of their careers.

Figure 35 - The difficult professional climb.

Many roles require employees to become proficient in new types of software or equipment. Employees benefit from structured learning programs and daily coaching at work. There are insights to be gained by seeing colleagues handle tricky situations gracefully (or not) and seeing how managers motivate their teams (or don't).

Someone who starts taking orders at a fast-food restaurant learns the art of dealing with difficult customers and staying "cool" under pressure.

Someone who starts out in IT answering questions in a help center absorbs technical knowledge that they continue to use when they become network administrators.

An inventory clerk who watches his or her manager solve logistical problems can apply these approaches in a future role as a warehouse manager or purchasing agent.

3.2 Work experience contributes 40 to 60% of a worker's human capital

Valuing and recognizing human capital as one of the main pillars of individual wealth are essential aspects in the current economic and social scenario. Studies show that human capital represents about two-thirds of an individual's total wealth, highlighting the importance of knowledge, skills and competencies acquired throughout life.

Among the factors that contribute significantly to the formation of this human capital, work experience stands out. Through experiences and learning in the professional environment, it is possible to acquire specific and generic skills that are fundamental for personal and professional development. It is estimated that work experience accounts for about 46% of the total value of human capital over the course of a typical career.

However, it is important to note that this percentage varies significantly depending on individual context and circumstances. The contribution of work experience to human capital can be influenced by several factors, such as the level of qualification, the area of expertise, the organizational environment, and the professional development opportunities available.

In this sense, it is essential that individuals are aware of the importance of work experience in building and valuing their human capital. Investing in learning opportunities, seeking challenges and projects that allow the development of new skills, and keeping up to date with trends and innovations in the labor market are essential strategies to enhance the contribution of professional experience to individual wealth.

Thus, by recognizing and valuing the importance of work experience as a catalyst for human capital growth and enhancement, individuals will be able to maximize their potential, expand their perspectives, and achieve greater success and fulfillment throughout their professional trajectories. The effect of the experiment looks strikingly similar among advanced economies.

The contribution of work experience to an individual's lifetime earnings and professional development is a crucial aspect to consider in the global economic landscape.

Data show that in the United States, work experience represents a significant portion, corresponding to 40% of average lifetime earnings. Similarly, in both Germany and the United Kingdom, work experience contributes approximately 43% of earnings over the course of a career.

These figures reflect the importance of work experience not only as a determining factor in building human capital but also as a driver of financial gains over the course of an individual's career.

The experience and learning acquired throughout the professional career have the potential to add value to a worker's performance and skills, directly reflecting on their ability to generate income and achieve greater financial stability.

Work experience is not only limited to the monetary aspect, but also plays an essential role in building professional identity, developing interpersonal and technical skills, expanding networking, and opening up new opportunities for growth and career progression.

However, it is important to note that the contribution of work experience to earnings can vary depending on several factors, such as the industry in which you work, the level of expertise, market demand, and the professional growth opportunities available in each country.

Thus, it is essential that professionals are aware of learning and development opportunities throughout their careers, constantly seeking to improve their skills and competencies to obtain financial gains and more solid and lasting professional achievements.

Thus, by recognizing and valuing the contribution of work experience to lifelong earnings, professionals will be able to enhance their professional growth and success, making the most of opportunities. By contrast, work experience contributes 58% of average lifetime earnings in India.

Access to education remains a key challenge in India — and with only 12% of the population having tertiary education as of 2020, work experience will be a more important driver of income for the workforce as a whole by default.

The relationship between levels of educational attainment, productivity and wage growth represents a key aspect in the context of emerging economies. In countries where levels of educational attainment are low but productivity and wages are rising from a modest starting point, lifetime earnings are assumed to follow similar patterns.

In these emerging economies, education plays a crucial role in upskilling and upskilling the workforce, and is a key determinant of productivity and economic development. As workers acquire new knowledge and competencies through education and work experience, they become more efficient and skilled to perform their duties, which in turn positively influences productivity and, consequently, lifelong financial gains.

In addition, wage growth from a low starting point can drive an upward earnings trajectory over the course of a career. As the economy develops and new job opportunities emerge, workers can benefit from increased demand for skilled professionals and appreciation of their skills.

However, it is important to note that the impact of education and productivity on lifetime earnings can vary according to the specific characteristics and challenges of each emerging economy. Thus, it is essential that educational and economic policies are developed and implemented in a strategic and sustainable manner, aiming to promote an environment conducive to professional growth and the valorization of human capital.

Thus, when considering the interconnection between education, productivity and wage growth in emerging economies, it is possible to envision a scenario of development and progress, where workers have the opportunity to achieve significant gains throughout their careers, contributing to the strengthening and consolidation of the local economy and to increasing the well-being of society as a whole.

Continued investment in the education and skills development of workers is essential to boost competitiveness, innovation and sustainable growth in emerging economies.

Improving educational levels, coupled with valuing and acknowledging work experience, plays a crucial role in training a skilled workforce that is adaptable to the demands of the global market. With ever-evolving lifetime earnings, workers have the opportunity to build strong and financially rewarding careers, contributing to individual and collective prosperity.

It is through the effective combination of education, productivity, and wage growth that emerging economies can strengthen their economic foundations, drive sustainable development, and improve the quality of life of their citizens. By prioritizing investment in human capital and valuing knowledge and skills, it is possible to build a promising and dignified future for present and future generations.

Therefore, building a more just, equitable, and prosperous society requires a continuous commitment to education, professional training, and personal development, aiming not only at economic growth, but also at people's well-being and fulfillment. Through effective policies and strategies, it is possible to drive lifetime gains and create opportunities for progress and success for all members of society in emerging economies.

Figure 36 – The difference that experience makes.

The reverse is often true for people who start out in occupations with lower educational requirements. They typically earn less over their lifetime, with most of it driven by work experience.

The income growth of a dishwasher who becomes a kitchen assistant responsible for food preparation and then becomes an assistant cook and eventually a *sous chef* is almost entirely fueled by techniques and tricks of the trade learned on the job.

In addition to allowing someone to gain skills, work experience gives that person a track record, which is valuable in itself for the signal it sends to potential future employers. This *life-long professional learning* is greatly enriched by the development of the soft skills involved in this learning.

HUMAN CAPITAL AT WORK

In the United States, for example, the size of the experience effect varies substantially among entry-level occupations. At the bottom of the physiotherapy segment, for example, are chiropractors.

Before treating patients, they must complete a chiropractic qualification program that can take three to five years, then pass a series of licensing exams. Your entry-level skills account for 85% of your lifetime earnings.

While higher educational attainment often correlates with higher lifetime earnings, some people defy the odds.

Someone who has attended shoddy schools and doesn't have any extracurricular education or training is starting out behind in the job market. Many employers rely on college degrees as a well-established sign of a candidate's employability.

However, educational disadvantage doesn't have to stop fate, at least not for everyone. In the United States, for example, our projections of lifetime earnings show a subset of people who beat the odds.

Educational disadvantage doesn't have to hold back life's gains—at least not for everyone.

Figure 37 – Human capital as a professional factor.

In every country there is a sizable contingent of people who are on track to move up one or more quintiles from their starting points in their careers. This applies to about one-third of workers in advanced economies.

30% in the United States, 32% in Germany and 34% in the United Kingdom and 23% of workers in India. In the United States, about 6.1% are on track to move from the bottom to the top quintile in earnings.

The up-and-coming mobile group seems to be accumulating work experience effectively that yields real benefits. Gains in soft skills and experience promote an accreditation that generates 60 to 80 percent of lifetime gains, but only 35 to 55 percent for those who have remained stagnant or lagging.

Unfortunately, many people are unable to make these leaps because of structural and social barriers, such as prejudices, the lasting effects of unequal education, and a lack of professional networks.

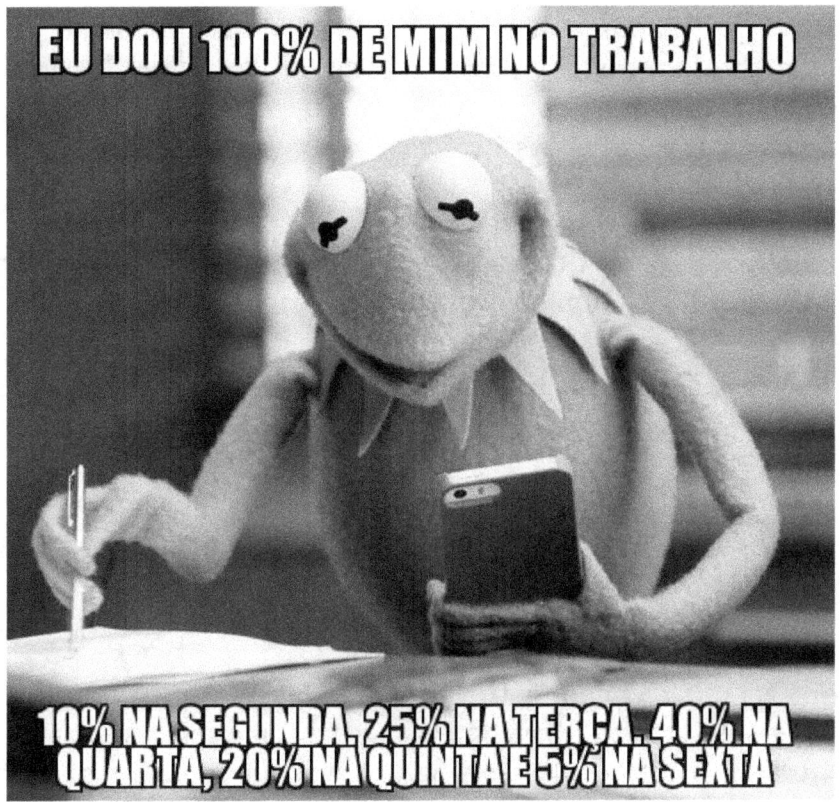

Figure 38 – The dedication of the professional.

Hat-swapping, the analogy commonly made in relation to swapping professional roles, has a beneficial effect on skills and can unlock higher earnings and open doors to moving to better positions.

Movement is an inherent characteristic of the labor market. Across the data set, the average person switched roles every two to four years, with a median skill gap of 25 to 45 percent, depending on the country. This matters because paper movements allow individuals to build or demonstrate their skills.

Movements may involve workers taking on new roles within their current company, moving to a different employer, changing specialties or occupations, or pursuing a combination of these strategies. At any given time, a significant proportion of role movements are triggered by layoffs and layoffs, as well as voluntary job changes.

Studies by organizations that monitor the labor market record data that indicate that these movements have increased wages by 6 to 10% on average. However, this includes people who have moved into lower-paying roles, either by choice or out of necessity.

Forty to 50% of the paper movements observed in the decade involved wage increases. Workers who made these moves were able to increase their earnings by 30 to 45 percent on average each time.

More than 80% of paper movements involve people moving from one employer to another.

More than 80% of role movements involve someone moving from one employer to another. Far fewer movements involved people being promoted into more senior roles or branching out into different specializations within their existing organizations.

This high level of movement is true across all layers. This seems to indicate that many employers don't have internal advancement ranges that are wide enough to keep most people growing and working toward higher rewards over time.

Individuals who want to reinvent themselves and take on more senior roles often have to go to a new environment to do so.

3.3   The bolder the movement, the greater the momentum.

The maxim "the bolder the move, the greater the momentum" reflects a fundamental principle in the professional and career landscape. Those who take the risk of taking on new challenges and roles that involve significant change are often rewarded with broader opportunities and benefits. By looking at the career trajectory of successful professionals, it is possible to see that role movements play a crucial role in an individual's professional evolution and growth.

HUMAN CAPITAL AT WORK

When someone decides to change jobs and take on a new position, it is common to notice that this change brings with it a number of challenges and skill requirements that are distinctly new from their previous position. These new challenges may include the need to acquire new skills, handle additional responsibilities, navigate new situations, and develop new ways of working and interacting with colleagues and leaders.

This dynamic of movement and career evolution not only stimulates the individual's personal and professional growth, but also opens doors to opportunities for learning, development, and progress. The courage to venture into new territories and take on more complex challenges can result in substantial rewards such as promotions, increased pay, professional recognition, and personal satisfaction.

However, it is important to emphasize that boldness and willingness to take on new challenges must be accompanied by strategic planning and a commitment to continuous development. It is essential to be prepared to face the obstacles and unforeseen events that arise along the way, constantly seeking to improve your skills, expand your knowledge, and strengthen your ability to adapt to changes in the job market.

By taking a proactive and bold stance towards their career, professionals can reap the rewards of their efforts and reach new heights of fulfillment and success. The willingness to challenge oneself and constantly seek new opportunities for growth not only drives professional development but also fuels a passion for work and the motivation to achieve increasingly ambitious goals.

Role moves in a career represent defining moments that can shape a professional's future and open doors to new and exciting possibilities. The decision to take on new roles and take on more complex challenges is a reflection of an individual's potential and determination to expand their horizons and pursue meaningful accomplishments in their professional life.

It is through the courage to take risks and the willingness to step out of their comfort zone that professionals can explore their full potential, acquire new experiences, and establish a lasting legacy in their respective areas of expertise. Each role move, no matter how challenging, represents a unique opportunity for growth and learning, allowing professionals to become more resilient, creative, and adaptable to the demands of the job market.

Therefore, when analyzing the career trajectory of professionals and observing the positive impacts of paper movements on their lives, it becomes evident that boldness and determination to take on new challenges are fundamental for personal and professional development. Those who are willing to launch themselves into the unknown and embrace opportunities for continuous growth are more likely to achieve success and fulfillment in their careers.

Wage increase movements involve a 35-50% skill gap between countries, greater than the 25-45% range for all movements between countries. In other words, when someone made a move for higher pay, their new job typically involved a more significant share of skills and responsibilities that weren't part of their previous job.

The new role can be a great learning opportunity, or it can be a better combination that allows someone to deploy existing skills that they haven't been using. Incremental moves with largely overlapping requirements don't pack the same ascent.

In the United States, for example, people who moved to higher-income quintiles had an average of 4.6 moves over a few years, while those who stayed in the same tier averaged 3.7 moves.

The upward movement in the U.S. and India demonstrates average skill gaps of 30 to 40 percent; Those who remained stabilized averaged only 20 to 30 percent.

This growth in skills compounds with each move, resulting in a much greater change in capabilities and responsibilities over the course of an entire working life.

HUMAN CAPITAL AT WORK

Figure 39 "Mafalda is the problem of right and wrong.

Employers can attract and retain talent by recognizing potential, embracing mobility, and empowering learning. But unfortunately, not all companies are equally good at developing people. Size is not the differentiator, as it is perceived that small businesses can be just as adept as their larger counterparts in this area.

But companies with the strongest organizational health, those that offer more structured training for their employees, and those that offer more opportunities for internal advancement seem to stand out. People join these companies to build knowledge and networking, understanding that their experience will provide a valuable signal to other employers for the remainder of their careers. Early career experience at these companies helps employees become more mobile.

Companies can help individuals grow—and establish themselves as great learning organizations and magnets for talent in the process.

Three priorities stand out, as described below.

3.3.1 Understand the potential in people, as well as their current knowledge and skills.

Most employers can benefit from challenging the *status quo* of how they select people for open roles.

The approach to recruitment and selection adopted by some of the leading organizations goes beyond simply matching candidates' previous experience with the responsibilities of the position in question.

Rather than merely looking for external candidates whose employment history is exactly aligned with the immediate demands of the open role, these innovative organizations have developed assessment systems that prioritize candidates' learnability, intrinsic skills, and transferable skills.

This paradigm shift in the selection process reflects a broader and deeper understanding that previous experience is not always the only or best indicator of success in a given position.

By recognizing that skills and competencies gained in previous roles can be transferable and adaptable to new challenges, organizations are betting on candidates with development and growth potential, rather than being tied to their work history alone.

Assessing candidates' ability to learn is a crucial aspect of this new recruitment model. The ability to absorb new knowledge, assimilate complex information and apply previous learning effectively can be a significant differential in the selection of professionals with potential for growth and career development.

In addition, valuing candidates' intrinsic skills, such as creativity, resilience, communication skills, and critical thinking, is essential to identify individuals with the ability to excel and bring innovation to the organization. These core competencies, often not measurable through prior experience, can be crucial for building diverse and dynamic teams.

The recognition of candidates' transferable skills, i.e., the ability to apply acquired knowledge and skills in diverse and challenging contexts, reveals a more comprehensive look at the potential of professionals to adapt and excel in new scenarios and work environments.

The implementation of more comprehensive and holistic evaluation systems in the candidate selection process reflects a long-term vision on the part of organizations, which seek to develop diverse and multifaceted teams, capable of facing the challenges of today's market in an innovative and effective way. By recognizing and valuing not only the past experience of professionals, but also their innate abilities and learning potential, companies are investing in strengthening their teams and fostering a dynamic and enriching work environment.

The ability to learn continuously and adapt to new contexts is an increasingly valued differential in the corporate world, where change and innovation are constant.

Professionals who demonstrate this ability to reinvent themselves and acquire new knowledge are more likely to stand out and progress in their careers, contributing to the success and competitiveness of organizations.

Additionally, by considering candidates' intrinsic skills, such as creativity, resilience, and the ability to solve complex problems, companies are strengthening their ability to address the challenges of the business world proactively and effectively.

These core competencies transcend previous professional experiences and are key to driving innovation and excellence at all levels of the organization.

By valuing the transferable skills of professionals, that is, the ability to apply knowledge and skills in different contexts, companies are promoting the versatility and adaptability of their employees. This approach not only enriches teams with different perspectives and experiences, but also strengthens the organization's ability to reinvent itself and stay relevant in an ever-changing market.

Valuing candidates' ability to learn, intrinsic skills, and transferable skills represents a significant shift in talent recruitment and selection practices, guiding organizations to adopt a more open, inclusive, and future-oriented approach.

By considering a candidate not only for their professional background, but also for their skills, growth potential, and adaptability, companies are building teams that are more resilient and prepared to face the challenges of the contemporary workplace.

This innovative approach to recruitment not only broadens the range of opportunities for professionals in career transition or looking for new challenges, but also fosters diversity and equal opportunities in the job market. By evaluating candidates based on broader, more inclusive criteria, organizations are promoting meritocracy and recognition of individual potential, regardless of background, gender, or prior experience.

The shift in focus to candidates' learnability, intrinsic skills, and transferable abilities reflects a mindset geared toward continuous development and innovation. The search for professionals who demonstrate versatility, creativity, and proactivity can drive innovation and excellence within companies, paving the way for new ideas and disruptive solutions.

By adopting more comprehensive and flexible assessment systems, leading organizations are redefining the standards of modern recruitment, prioritizing the growth potential and cultural fit of candidates with specific technical skills. This visionary approach not only benefits professionals looking for new opportunities, but also strengthens companies, making them more agile, diverse, and prepared to face the challenges of the future with resilience and innovation.

This requires designing fit-for-purpose assessments, focusing on the few fundamental skills that matter for success in the role.

3.3.2 Embrace mobility.

Since there's no way to prevent talent from leaving the organization, the key for employers is to become part of that flow. Employers can try to beat the odds on both sides of this 80-20 dynamic.

On the one hand, they can attract the best candidates among the great talent they are always looking for. On the other hand, they can increase the productivity and engagement of valuable employees who stay.

To ensure that talented employees don't have to go elsewhere to advance, organizations should set the expectation that part of a manager's job is to develop people who will go on to other activities. Each role should have clear pathways to future roles, with skill requirements outlined at each step.

One way to do this in a large organization is to create an internal digital platform where employees can access learning modules and find their next opportunity. Mobility is experience, not just upward progression.

Lateral movement is an overlooked opportunity for many organizations. When talented employees move on, celebrate them as success stories and don't close the door on welcoming them back in a different capacity in the future.

3.3.3 Strengthen coaching, especially at the beginning of an employee's tenure.

A great deal of skill development happens on a day-to-day basis at work. Coaching and learning can maximize this effect.

The first few years of a career, and similarly the first year in a new job, play an essential role in employee professional development and onboarding.

The transition to a new work environment, with its dynamics, organizational culture and specific challenges, can be a decisive moment to establish the foundations of a lasting and productive relationship between the professional and the company.

In this sense, the formal onboarding process should not be seen as just a simple orientation session, but as an ongoing period, which extends over six months to a year, and which involves a carefully planned and executed journey.

Effective onboarding goes far beyond the presentation of the company's policies, procedures, and organizational structure. It should provide complete immersion in the work environment, facilitating the integration of the new employee into the culture and values of the organization, as well as their role and responsibilities within the team.

Throughout this period of adaptation, the professional has the opportunity to get to know the company, their colleagues and their projects in depth, which contributes to them feeling an integral part of the team and aligned with the organization's objectives and values.

The onboarding journey should be structured in such a way as to promote not only the integration of the employee, but also their professional and personal development. Through mentoring, training, and regular feedback, the company can provide the necessary support so that the new team member feels comfortable, confident, and empowered to perform their duties with excellence.

In addition, onboarding can be a good time to set clear goals, identify opportunities for growth, and establish an individualized development plan for the professional.

By investing in a comprehensive and well-structured onboarding, organizations not only facilitate the onboarding of new employees, but also promote the engagement, retention, and development of talent within the company.

HUMAN CAPITAL AT WORK

An effective onboarding process involves a comprehensive approach that goes beyond simply welcoming the new employee, but also encompasses building interpersonal relationships, aligning expectations, and creating an environment conducive to mutual development and success.

During the first months in a new work environment, the employee is in a phase of adaptation and absorption of information. It is during this period that he develops a deeper understanding of organizational culture, internal processes, and performance expectations.

Well-structured onboarding provides the necessary tools and resources for the employee to integrate effectively, allowing them to feel part of the team and find their space within the company.

In addition, continuous onboarding plays a crucial role in employee development, providing support and guidance so that they can acquire new skills, expand their knowledge, and reach their full potential.

Through mentoring, personalized training and constructive feedback, professionals can grow and evolve in their careers, contributing significantly to the company's success.

On the other hand, organizations that invest in solid and consistent onboarding reap the rewards of an engaged, motivated, and prepared team to face market challenges. Valuing the new employee from the first steps in the work environment creates a positive organizational climate, favoring talent retention and contributing to the construction of a high-performance culture.

In short, formal onboarding and the carefully crafted journey that comes with it are not just elements of onboarding, but powerful tools to promote mutual success between employee and company. By investing in this process of welcoming and developing new professionals, companies reinforce their position in the market, strengthen their team and build the foundations for a promising and sustainable future.

Organizations can provide the tools for an ongoing adaptation process by including a manager who is committed to providing coaching and facilitating connections.

Even after being adapted and integrated into the company, employees need continuous opportunities to learn. This results in increased team morale and reduced attrition.

In a June 2021 Gallup poll, 65% of U.S. workers said learning new skills is an extremely or very important factor in deciding whether to take a new job, and 61% said it was extremely or very important to decide whether to stay in their current job.

HUMAN CAPITAL AT WORK

By recognizing and investing in human capital development, companies are building a strong foundation for long-term success, as it is the talents and skills of professionals that drive innovation and growth."

Harvard Business Review

4 THE NECESSARY KNOWLEDGE THAT EVERY PROFESSIONAL IN THE MODERN WORLD SHOULD HAVE.

Technical knowledge is essential to carry out any activity in a company. Companies, when selecting their candidates, expect everyone who is vying for the position to have the knowledge previously required.

But what we see is not exactly like that, because unfortunately we receive numerous resumes of professionals in companies, without any conditions of hiring. They are people, totally misaligned with the requirements for the position, totally unprepared in the aspect of technical knowledge and even without a profession.

Over the years, a professional's technical knowledge has undergone a continuous process of development and improvement, reflecting the evolutions and demands of the labor market. A clear example of this progress is the personal history of many professionals, who at the beginning of their careers may have acquired technical skills that, over time, have become obsolete or less relevant.

The account of entering the first job with the knowledge of typing as a highlight in the resume illustrates well how technical skills can transform over time. In the past, typing was an essential skill for office professionals and was even considered a differentiator in the job market.

However, with the advancement of technology and the popularization of computers and word processing software, typing has ceased to be a fundamental skill for most professions.

Nowadays, companies are looking for professionals with skills that are more in line with contemporary demands, such as knowledge of specific software, digital skills, critical thinking, problem-solving, and teamwork. The focus on developing skills relevant to the current work environment is essential to keep up with the constant transformations of the market and to remain competitive and professionally updated.

Thus, the professional who enters the job market today needs to be aware of the importance of keeping up with constant learning and evolution, investing in skills that are valued by companies and that are aligned with the trends of the sector in which they operate.

The search for current and pertinent technical knowledge, combined with behavioral and emotional skills, becomes fundamental for success and career progression.

In an increasingly dynamic and competitive landscape, professionals need to be willing to adapt, learn new skills, and keep up with changes in the job market to stay relevant and achieve professional success.

Investing in the constant development of technical knowledge and continuous improvement of skills is essential to keep up with the rapid pace of technological transformations and business models.

Companies increasingly value professionals who are versatile, adaptable, and have the ability to reinvent themselves, demonstrating not only technical knowledge, but also skills such as creativity, critical thinking, and the ability to innovate.

The history of typing as an essential skill in the past and obsolete in the present is a powerful reminder of the importance of adaptation and continuous evolution in the job market. Those who settle into their technical skills and don't invest in new learning run the risk of becoming outdated and less competitive in an ever-changing landscape.

Therefore, it is essential that professionals are open to acquiring new skills, seeking continuous training, and staying up-to-date on trends and innovations in their areas of expertise. Investment in education and personal development becomes an increasingly relevant differentiator for individuals who want to remain competitive and advance in their careers.

In addition, businesses also play a key role in fostering an environment that is conducive to continuous learning and innovation. Training, mentoring, coaching, and leadership development programs are essential to provide employees with the tools and opportunities they need to grow and develop professionally.

The history of typing as an outdated skill in the current context illustrates the importance of continuous learning and adaptation in the job market. Those who constantly seek to update themselves, hone their skills, and nurture a growth mindset are more likely to excel, evolve, and thrive in an ever-changing and evolving professional environment.

Many professionals still insert in their resumes, information with their qualifications in computer science, mentioning a list of programs ranging from text editors to graphic programs, some of which are totally inapplicable to the function claimed by the professional.

It is necessary to understand that knowing how to use a text editor or prepare a spreadsheet is no longer any differential, because if you are going to carry out an administrative activity, it is a prerequisite that you know all this, so do not mention a list of courses you have taken, just describe that you have mastery in computer science.

Using this same example, what has been observed in many professionals, who even use the computer for years, is what I call a lay computer operator. The lay computer operator is that professional who only knows how to do the basics on his computer, not understanding anything else.

Often the person who didn't even have the ability to press the esc key when the computer stopped at a screen that wasn't the one the operator expected. Therefore, increase your technical knowledge in order to know beyond the basics, and the best way to do this is what "informaniacs" would call "poking around". Therefore, learn more about this subject in order to better understand the existing technologies.

However, the knowledge is not restricted exclusively to the computer domains, as it involves the technical areas of professional activity.

In this respect, knowledge has been developing, and the technical skills required for the professional in the modern world go far beyond simply learning to operate a machine, as he now has to learn how to program the machine.

Likewise, it is not enough for him to be just a practitioner, for he must know the technical fundamentals of the work to be performed.

Still Speaking of up-to-date knowledge for the performance of their functions in the company, the most widespread way to obtain knowledge today is the school. There is a vast number of higher and technical courses available to professionals, lectures, workshops and so on.

Since the offer of courses is large, professionals must carefully choose the course they will take. There is now a very large availability of motivational speeches, which are able to raise the self-esteem of professionals, but are poor in terms of "content". Personally, I don't discriminate against this type of lectures, but I understand that professionals should be careful not to focus their training only on Thatso that they do not become highly motivated professionals, without, however, essential technical qualifications.

There are many qualified companies when it comes to training with highly up-to-date programs that are applicable to the needs of the market.

Thus, we will highlight the main options available in the pursuit of the knowledge of the successful professional of the modern world.

4.1 Higher course.

We are starting to talk directly about higher education, since this has become a prerequisite for most of the vacancies available in the job market. Today, large companies are requiring service professionals in telemarketing centers to have a degree or are attending a higher level. This shows that every day, the college degree is being the passport for your resume to be accepted in the company, without directly meaning a hiring.

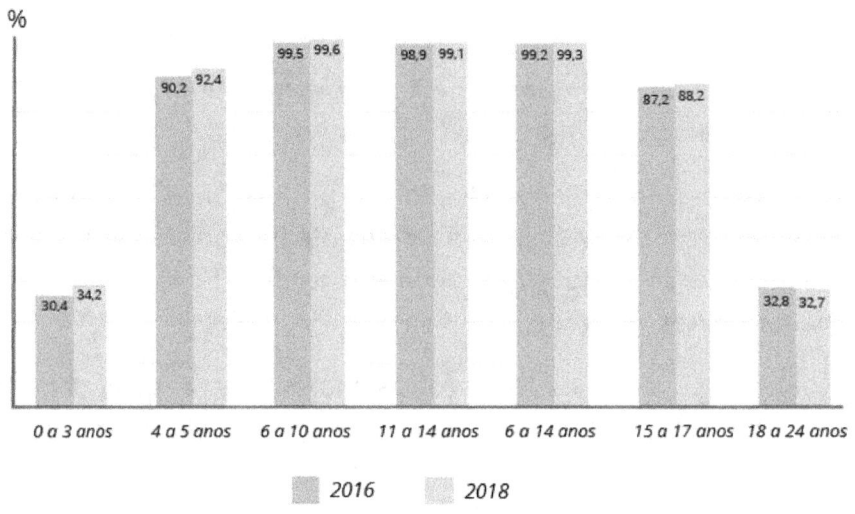

Figure 40- Access to higher education.

A few years ago, the technical course diploma was enough, but even so, I consider that for the minor who is entering the job market, having a technical level training is highly recommended, but always remembering that the technical college does not replace the higher education.

There are currently higher education courses aimed at specific or technological training, lasting two to three years. This can be an advantage for the professional, because instead of taking four, five or more years to obtain a comprehensive view of a particular profession, he can have a more focused education and then take a postgraduate degree, thus being able, at the same time as a bachelor's degree, to have two diplomas: one technological or sequential degree and one postgraduate degree.

This type of higher education course has become a fever in many countries and has been very well accepted by Brazilian companies, in addition to being a possibility of quick training for those who need a higher education and have been in the job market for years.

In any case, don't forget to seek your professional training through a degree, otherwise your chances of success will be greatly reduced in the job market.

4.2 Postgraduate studies.

As the higher education course has become a prerequisite, what can help you is to have a differential is the postgraduate degree. This is essential, for example, in specific areas where only a degree usually does not bring a differential, such as lawyers, administrators, among others. It is much easier for a lawyer who is a graduate to achieve a competitive advantage than one who has not attended a graduate degree.

In addition, graduate courses in general are quick and will not require as much effort and time to complete, and can be taken on just two days a week or on weekends. The same application to postgraduate courses also applies to MBA (Master in Business Administration) courses, which a few years ago became a fever among professionals and companies, taking over the whole country.

When it comes to MBA, what we have in Brazil is a real salad of meanings, but to put it simply, we can say that they exist today:

- Executive Master's MBA that follows the North American standard, which is a postgraduate degree with the same requirements as the academic master's degree, and few universities offer this in Brazil;
- Executive MBA in which most Brazilian MBAs belong to this category, which gives the student a generalist training in business management and is aimed at professionals with certain professional experiences;
- MBA, which is nothing more than specialization courses without a generalist focus and that use the acronym MBA, due to the strong commercial appeal it gives.

It is not our intention to judge the qualifications of existing MBAs, but given the enormity of courses offered, it is up to the professional to be well-informed about the qualification of the course, as well as the institution that offers it.

HUMAN CAPITAL AT WORK

Having an MBA in the curriculum can be an important differential for the professional, because in addition to the strong curricular appeal, it will give a baggage of differentiated knowledge, since the main characteristic of the MBA is precisely the practical focus of the application of knowledge, having a program rich in case studies and its applicability in the real environment.

Given this, we can conclude that a graduate degree or an MBA gives the professional a competitive advantage, but it is not everything, as we will see in the next chapter.

Although we talk about graduation and obtaining knowledge through courses, training, lectures, among others, we cannot forget to mention the importance of reading for professional improvement.

It is worth noting that the criteria for choosing titles for reading, given the vast availability that exists, makes it difficult to make a decision about which one to purchase. Therefore, it is important that the professional is also judicious, since the availability of books of little use is great. You will be able to look at the title of the book, paying attention to its content and analyze if it is suitable for your needs. In several areas of activity, if not in all, there are authors usually qualified as "gurus" of the subject, who represent the books of "mandatory reading".

Finally, also complement your knowledge by reading specialized publications, newspapers, magazines and other subjects of personal interest outside the technical context, because it is not enough to have only technical knowledge, without also knowing other subjects, usually not related to the professional aspect. The quadrant below demonstrates what the development of professional knowledge can look like.

CONHECIMENTO TÉCNICO ↑	Alto nível de conhecimento técnico e baixo de conhecimento de assuntos gerais (DESEJAVEL)	Alto nível de conhecimento técnico e assuntos gerais (ALTAMENTE DESEJAVEL)
	Baixo nível de conhecimento técnico e de conhecimento de assuntos gerais (INDESEJAVEL)	Alto nível de conhecimento de assuntos gerais e baixo de conhecimento técnico (DESEJAVEL)
	CONHECIMENTO DE ASSUNTOS GERAIS →	

Figure 41 – Knowledge quadrant.

As noted in the quadrant above, the professional should possess an excellent level of technical knowledge, but should not disregard the importance of knowledge of general subjects, which include the information obtained from other readings as already mentioned, as well as through television programs, travel, and so on.

Another preponderant factor in defining the professional knowledge that you should dedicate yourself to is precisely the hierarchical degree that you are or will want to be in the organization.

For this, the rule is that the higher the hierarchical level, the greater the degree of vision of the whole, that is, the level of specialization of knowledge will be more applicable to the lower hierarchical levels, while the professionals of higher hierarchical levels will need more generalist or conceptual knowledge of the business.

This explains why top executives often switch organizations to totally different segments than the previous ones and are still successful, because they have a systemic view of the business that can be applied to other businesses in different branches.

Figure 42 – Structure of hierarchical levels.

1. Low hierarchical level.

Production, sales and other personnel – As this is a low hierarchical level, a high level of technical knowledge is required for the activities performed, usually focused only on the specific function. Such professionals tend to be totally unaware of the conceptual aspects of the business, but have knowledge focused on the execution of tasks.

2. Middle Hierarchical Level.

Supervisor – Good level of technical knowledge, but with a broader vision. They are usually professionals who have already held low-level positions and have a practical vision. From this pillar we start to value skills in human resources management.

Management – Medium level of technical knowledge in production processes and medium level in the conceptualization aspects of the business in which the company operates. Skills related to human resource management are no longer desirable but necessary, since such professionals are now directly linked to teams.

3. High hierarchical level.

Directors – Low level of technical knowledge of the production process as a whole, medium level of human resources skills, and high conceptual level of the business. These are the professionals who understand the business in which they are including the external environmental factors that directly or indirectly influence the company, even if they are often unaware of the details of how the tasks are performed.

The model clearly demonstrates that as you rise to intermediate levels of management and supervision, you should possess human resources skills that enable you to deal with people, while as you reach the C-suite levels, you should also possess conceptual knowledge of the business.

But don't forget that the responsibility for professional development lies primarily with you, so you have to continually seek self-development.

4.3 Is the professional desired by companies an entrepreneur?

The days of the employee who behaves as an employee may be numbered. The traditionalist view of employer and employee, boss and subordinate are moving into disuse.

Companies with a modern vision are looking at their employees as collaborators or partners and implementing the entrepreneurial vision. This means that entrepreneurs have realized that giving employees the possibility of earning more than simply the fixed monthly salary has been a good business, as it makes the professional make greater contributions to the organization, thus ensuring the commitment of the team in the search for positive results.

The practice of rewarding people for their work has existed since the early days of the capitalist system of production, but it was after the First World War that a standard of rewards was established. Nowadays, variable compensation is most often linked to performance and the performance of the professional in relation to the results presented to their respective organizations.

In addition to all this, it can be said that the greatest competitive advantage of organizations is not the machines, equipment or technology used, but the people.

We can study the biggest business success stories and we will confirm it. But I would just like to use the example of one of the most prominent companies in the world, which is Starbucks, which has managed to differentiate a commodity, coffee, and has become the largest and most profitable coffee retailer in the world.

It achieved this not by investing heavily in marketing, as these were much smaller compared to companies of similar size, but by investing in people, making them entrepreneurs by offering profit-sharing options and even equity stakes to employees.

The results are highly rewarding for the company, as it manages to create an emotional bond with the people who work there and as a result, they start to collaborate with innovative ideas for the company. Starbucks, an American company famous for its coffees, takes all this so seriously that the people who work there, since 1991, are no longer called employees but "partners".

Although these human resources policies are nonsensical in the business world for most companies, the tendency is that successful companies will be those whose employees have this entrepreneurial profile, being effectively committed to the company. That is why we can understand that in companies there are two types of employees: Those who participate in the company (are engaged) and those who attend the company (only commit).

In the same way, companies like Correios would not achieve the results they have achieved in parcel transport, only with excellent logistics without the commitment of the people who are there. And the examples multiply.

Well, what does all this mean for you professional?

This means that to become a successful professional, you need to be and act like an entrepreneur. Those who have been entrepreneurs know that entrepreneurial activities are not easy at all. The entrepreneur knows that in order to be successful, he will have to manage his company in a rational way.

Employees who play their respective roles in the company must temper the performance of their duties with an entrepreneurial profile, contributing to improvements in the company.

This means knowing as deeply as possible the company's strategies, goals, vision, and mission.

It means being attuned to the company's interests, showing personal interest, and making contributions to the company. Become a consultant and advisor in your field and your chances of success will be noticeably higher.

Good companies value professionals who are committed to the business, while "regulars" are the first to be replaced.

But what if your company doesn't allow this participation? Well, in this case, rest assured that the problem is with the company and not with you, and it will hardly survive in the face of all the business challenges that exist in the modern world.

Successful companies know that one of the main factors for success is valuing people, as they are the ones who play the main role in customer loyalty.

4.4   A network also influences your knowledge.

Building a networking network has become a key tool for professionals today.

But don't think that building a relationship network means going up or down handing out cards at random, even though the exchange of cards, paper or digital, is an important factor in building a database of professionals, like you.

Building a networking network involves much more than that, as it involves earning the respect of other professionals and offering them something in return instead of just taking advantage of contacts.

Despite the benefits, what I've noticed is that people give very little value to this, as if being successful professionally is something similar to a race where there is only one runner – you – when in reality it's not like that.

Figure 43 – A good network can make all the difference.

In the professional business world, we have to build relationships with our peers, subordinates, superiors, and even with people who are totally unconnected to your current professional career, but who may in one way or another indicate you.

Replacing yourself in the job market will bring greater opportunities if you have a good network. The relationship network basically works as a factor for indicating the professional for projects, opportunities for advancement and new jobs.

In today's job market, the "IQ" factor has become an increasingly common and relevant practice for hiring professionals in companies of different sizes and segments.

The influence of networking and personal recommendations in legitimizing a hire is a trend that is growing as organizations seek qualified professionals who are a good fit for the work environment and the demands of the company.

"IQ" is an element that goes beyond the candidate's technical skills and resume, it involves other people's perception of the skills, values, and behavior of the professional in question.

Often, referrals made by colleagues, managers, business partners or mentors can be considered as an important endorsement of the candidate's ability and suitability, facilitating the hiring process and increasing the company's confidence in choosing the new employee.

For large companies, the "IQ" factor can represent an effective way to filter the sheer volume of candidates applying for jobs, allowing recruiters to rely on personal references to find talent that stands out from the competition. In addition, recommendations from internal or external professionals can provide a better cultural fit and a smoother integration of the new employee into the team.

In small companies, where proximity and interpersonal relationships can be even more valued, the "IQ" factor gains even more relevance. Trust between team members and the business owner's or manager's network of contacts can be decisive in hiring new talent that fits the company's culture and needs.

However, although the "IQ" factor can be a common and effective practice in the job market, it is important to emphasize that the technical competence and skills of the professional should not be disregarded. The recommendation of strong networking can open doors and facilitate the selection process, but it does not replace the importance of objective assessment of the candidate's skills and experiences.

It is essential for companies to adopt transparent and fair recruitment practices, ensuring that hiring is based on merit and the professional's suitability for the requirements of the position.

The "IQ" factor can be a valuable way to obtain additional information about the candidate and to validate their qualifications, but it should be used as a complement rather than the sole selection criterion. It is essential that companies carry out a thorough evaluation of all candidates, taking into account not only the indications but also the knowledge, skills and attitudes necessary for the effective performance of the roles.

Additionally, organizations should seek to promote diversity and inclusion in the recruitment process, ensuring equal opportunities for all candidates, regardless of personal referrals or recommendations. The search for diverse and qualified talent enriches the team, fosters innovation, and contributes to a more collaborative and dynamic work environment.

Thus, while the "IQ" factor can be a facilitator in hiring professionals, it is essential that companies value impartiality, transparency, and meritocracy in their selection processes. By balancing the influence of personal recommendations with the objective assessment of competencies, organizations can ensure more assertive hires, engaged employees, and a more productive and inclusive work environment.

In order for networking to really have the desired effect, it is important to know some essential points that we will address below:

- SELECTIVITY. Try to cultivate your network with people who can really contribute to you. This is important, because some people, whether for social, hierarchical, or other reasons, will not be able to contribute anything at all professionally. That is why the most beneficial thing is to maintain selective relationships and preferably with managers, supervisors, directors, human resources professionals and other professionals who have weight in a nomination, whatever it may be.

- INFORMATION. Keep your network well-informed about your professional growth. When people are familiar with your professional qualifications and follow all your professional achievements, they will feel motivated to refer you to be part of the professional staff of the company they work for. This is due to the fact that if your hiring is beneficial to the company, the person who referred you will be honored. There is always the fear that we will refer a person and that person will not meet the expectations we present to the indicated company. In this way, when your contacts get to know your professional qualifications better, this will provide greater security for your referrals.
- RELATIONSHIP. Have a good relationship with other professionals. No one would point out someone who only brings trouble wherever he goes. As we have already said, companies look for professionals who know how to relate to other professionals. For this reason, the better you are at this, the more people will be attracted to approach you. And this will be a differential for possible indications. Just look at the following fact. If you had to nominate a good professional in the technical aspect, but with an unprofessional profile in the personal aspect, that is, a perfect troublemaker, would you indicate it? Most likely not.
- ATTITUDE. Never look down on another professional's company. If there's one thing that tarnishes the image, it's the bad habit of talking disparagingly about another professional's company. Of course, some companies, even the employees who work in them, speak badly, but when you talk badly about the company in your network, they will understand, that they should never invite you to work there. Therefore, in many cases, it is more prudent to remain silent than to engage in such conversations.

If you are an entrepreneur or a self-employed professional, networking is equally important to cultivate. Many deals can come about through a simple exchange of cards. On any given day, one of these contacts might come to you simply because they had a card from you.

Networking will be much more successful if it's a two-way street. We need to make a positive contribution to others, so that we can make a contribution when needed. Therefore, we can say that creating relationships does not only mean taking advantage of contacts when you need to, but also gradually contributing to these relationships with a view to the future.

"A company's true competitive advantage is in the hands and minds of its employees. Human capital is the key to driving productivity, creativity and innovation in the workplace."

Deloitte

5 KNOWLEDGE. YOUR HUMAN CAPITAL.

Knowledge is the human capacity to understand, apprehend and comprehend things, moreover it can be applied, creating and experiencing the new.

Knowledge is the human ability to grasp something. From what is learned, one can create, as the sciences and the arts do.

5.1 Meaning of knowledge

The word knowledge originates from the Latin word cognoscere, which means "act of knowing". Knowing, in Latin, also comes from the same root "gno", present in the Latin language and in ancient Greek, from the word "gnosis", which means knowledge, or "gnostic", which is the one who knows.

Figure 44 –Knowledge.

Knowing is the act of apprehending, of being able to abstract laws of understanding and understand something. Knowledge is the attribute of the one who knows, that is, it is that which results from the act of knowing, understanding, etc.

Knowledge is made up of 3 basic elements:

1. The subject (or knower): the person capable of obtaining knowledge.

2. The object (or knowable): what or what can be known.

3. Representation: which is the subject's understanding of the object.

For you to understand in a practical way, these elements work as follows: you are the subject, this text you are reading is the object, and the representation is what you are understanding of it.

There are also two main theories that explain the origin of knowledge, i.e., how it arises:

1. Empiricism: explains that knowledge is acquired from experience, from the subject's contact with the world.

2. Rationalism: explains that all knowledge comes through reason, the simple act of thinking.

Knowledge is possible only to human beings. Animals, on the other hand, develop learning mechanisms through practical experience and the repetition of experiences, but complex, effective and rational knowledge is only apprehended by us.

This is because the well-structured knowledge we develop can only be elaborated, organized, codified and decoded by language and our rational mechanisms (language and reasoning are necessarily interconnected elements, and it is impossible to determine which has arisen first in human beings, since there is an interdependence between both).

5.2 What are the types of knowledge

Since language was developed, human beings have sought mechanisms to know and establish relationships between the world and their experiences with it, trying to demystify and understand the complexity of existence. For this reason, we have developed, over ten millennia or so, various ways of understanding the world, which attests to the existence of several different types of knowledge.

5.2.1 Common sense knowledge

It is one of the most comprehensive types of human knowledge, as it is based on private and social experiences, shared through exchanges of experiences and hereditary relationships. Common sense knowledge is based on popular wisdom and the expression of opinions, and can have a value and importance because it is closely linked to cultural formation.

Common sense knowledge can also manifest true beliefs and opinions, but it is necessary to be careful with this type of knowledge when you want something to base yourself on and affirm with certainty, because common sense knowledge does not require any type of validation or method that attests to its rational logical sense or its veracity.

5.2.2 Theological knowledge

This kind of knowledge also inhabits society and the particular ways of human life, since the human being seeks religion from the beginning to explain what is, so far, inexplicable. We can establish two marks within the record of theological knowledge.

One of them is religion itself, which human beings seek as a form of comfort and "supernatural" explanation, and the other is the record of Theology, as a branch of scientific knowledge that tries to create a structure of facts and elements that make up religions. Theological knowledge, as a religion in itself, is based on the personal faith that people manifest and on elements of the religion itself, with scriptures, practices, rituals, dogmas, beliefs, etc.

5.2.3 Philosophical knowledge

Philosophy emerged as a set of knowledge necessary to question and, at times, complement the knowledge provided by common sense and religion. Philosophy is a way of establishing norms for obtaining a safer type of knowledge, just like science, but we cannot say that scientific knowledge happens in the same way as philosophical knowledge. Philosophy, in this sense, is the mother of all sciences, for it was the first to seek a way of knowing things more surely.

5.2.4 Scientific knowledge

This type, in turn, must be rigorously tested and verified, which guarantees it greater veracity. This causes us to look to science to determine valid and correct ways of thinking, so that we do not easily fall into error.

The activity of the scientist, especially those who dedicate themselves to the natural sciences, is fundamental for the advancement of knowledge and understanding of the world around us.

Close observation of natural phenomena, identification of patterns and discrepancies, formulation of hypotheses, and conducting experiments to test these hypotheses are essential steps in the process of scientific inquiry.

By observing and analyzing the phenomena of nature, scientists seek to understand the laws and principles that govern the functioning of the universe, from physical and chemical processes to biological and environmental phenomena.

From the identification of problems and gaps in existing knowledge, scientists formulate hypotheses that seek to explain the observed phenomena and predict future results.

The experimental testing phase is crucial to validate or refute the hypotheses formulated. Controlled, systematic experiments allow scientists to collect data, analyze results, and evaluate the validity of their theories. The accuracy and reproducibility of the experiments are essential to ensure the reliability of the results and the construction of a solid and grounded knowledge.

Based on the results obtained, scientists are able to formulate logical deductions and draw conclusions about the observed phenomena. Based on these conclusions, it is possible to advance in the construction of theories and explanatory models that comprehensively and coherently represent the laws and principles that govern the natural world.

Thus, it is through the rigorous scientific method, which involves observation, experimentation, hypothesis formulation, testing, and deductions, that scientists expand human knowledge, expand the frontiers of knowledge, and contribute to the progress of humanity.

Science is a continuous process of inquiry and discovery, which allows us to unravel the mysteries of nature, develop new technologies, and seek solutions to the challenges and problems we face as a society.

Scientific activity is characterized by constant questioning, by the incessant search for truth and innovation. Scientists are always searching for answers to the riddles of the universe, challenging established concepts, proposing new approaches, and reformulating theories in light of new discoveries.

Moreover, science is not only limited to the discovery of natural facts and laws, but also plays a crucial role in our understanding of the world and improving the quality of life. Through scientific research, we are able to develop new technologies, find solutions to complex problems and promote advances in various areas, such as medicine, ecology, engineering and computer science.

However, it is important to emphasize that scientific practice must be guided by ethical values, transparency, and responsibility. The replicability of experiments, honesty in the collection and interpretation of data, and unbiased disclosure of results are fundamental to the credibility and reliability of science as a whole.

Therefore, the task of the scientist goes far beyond the simple investigation of natural phenomena; It involves a commitment to the pursuit of knowledge, the promotion of critical thinking, and contributing to the advancement of society as a whole. It is through dedication and scientific rigor that we can expand our horizons, solve complex challenges, and build a more promising and sustainable future for all.

5.2.5 Knowledge for Philosophy

Since its inception, Philosophy has dealt with the question of knowledge, since it arises to present a new way of knowing the world. Throughout their history, philosophers have presented different theories about the way human beings know and the ways of knowing themselves.

If we take into consideration knowledge in antiquity, Plato admits the existence of only two degrees of knowledge: the sensible and the intelligible. The sensible, caused by data from the bodily senses, was inferior and deceptive, while the intelligible was rational and superior.

Aristotle, on the other hand, establishes a mixture of several different degrees of knowledge that must necessarily pass through sensible knowledge in order to awaken information in the person. The theories of these two thinkers influenced the entire debate on knowledge held by later philosophers.

The ways of knowing gave rise to the field of Philosophy called Epistemology, which formulates the basis of the theory of knowledge. Another area that emerges is the Philosophy of Science, which seeks to problematize the issue of scientific method and knowledge, providing advances for the use of science itself.

If we consider the historical issues within the Philosophy of Science, we have the moment, in Modernity, when Galileo Galilei, for the first time, dedicated himself to explaining the need to achieve a method to achieve scientific knowledge.

However, the clash over knowledge that most marked Modernity was the quarrel between empiricists and rationalists. The empiricists held that knowledge is obtained only through practical and sensible experience, which by means of the data obtained by the sense organs and sent to the brain produce ideas.

The leading empiricists who are advocating experience as a way to access true knowledge are John Locke and David Hume.

Figure 45 - John Locke is an important figure of modern empiricism.

Rationalists, on the other hand, argued that the origin of knowledge is purely rational and intellectual, not necessarily affected by the external environment. René Descartes, on the other hand, is a rationalist philosopher who argues that true knowledge is solely and exclusively the work of our reasoning, and that we should be suspicious of any kind of knowledge coming from the senses of the body, because these, according to Descartes, could deceive us.

Paul Feyerabend, a twentieth-century philosopher of science, contrary to the previous tradition, dedicated himself to defending an anarchist science, free of fixed methods and rules, more open to plurality and creativity. In his book Science in a Free Society, the contemporary thinker speaks of the importance of freeing scientific work from methods and constraints, which has generated criticism and an intense debate in the field of Philosophy of Science and science itself.

Thomas Kuhn, also a contemporary philosopher and scholar of epistemology, was an intense critic of Feyerabend's work, as he believed that the essential thing about science was the reliability of its method.

Friedrich Nietzsche founded a new epistemological strand that he called perspectivism, which defends the non-possibility of the positivist claim to base knowledge, especially in the Social Sciences and History, on facts, because what happens is narrated from perspectives.

The book published in 1874, entitled On the Usefulness and Disadvantage of History for Life (the second book that the philosopher released in a series of four writings entitled Extemporaneous Considerations) centralizes Nietzsche's critique of the historical knowledge made until then, based on the search for facts, but without realizing that a fact can have the version or interpretation of one or more people who experienced an event.

5.2.6 Faith.

It seems that nowadays there is a certain common sense among us that faith and knowledge are opposite, mutually exclusive things like light and darkness – if you have knowledge you have no faith, and vice versa.

There is, however, to counter this notion, a very forceful statement in the Bhagavad-Gita about the relationship between these two principles: "shraddhavan labhate jnanam – he who has faith gains knowledge." According to Krishna, the author of this statement, knowledge and faith are not only not opposites, but maintain a very peculiar relationship of dependence between them: faith is the sine qua non of knowledge. Let's understand what this means.

First of all, what is knowledge? It seems to me that it is something whose force of evidence dispels any doubts or misgivings about what is showing itself so clearly, and makes it possible for us to relax and go on with whatever we are doing without thinking about it any further.

Right now as I write this text there is a huge amount of knowledge involved in this action, one of the most essential of which is that the words are actually being written in the word processor, which allows me to relax and just write. And what is it that gives me the certainty that in fact the words are being written? They are my eyes, with which I have a relationship of full trust, faith.

I give my eyes the status of being valid means of knowledge with respect to the shape and color of things. And the only thing that makes me stand up for this status is my good faith.

It is no other organ of perception that validates or proves the authority of my eyes. If I showed you a black object and asked what color the object is, you would answer me correctly: black. And if I then asked you to prove to me that the object is black, what would you do? How would you prove it?

It is clear that no sense organ other than the eyes can say anything about color, nor can logic do so. What reasoning could you develop to prove or deny the fact that the object is black? None, because color is the subject of the eye only, and the eye is the sole and sufficient proof for colors.

Having faith that my eyes are a valid means of knowledge, I can interact with the world reasonably well. And if I didn't have that faith, what would become of me? There are many people in the world with a faith disorder called Obsessive-Compulsive Disorder, OCD.

There are many degrees of manifestation of this disorder, and in the most serious cases the person is, for example, washing his hands for hours, believing that they are dirty even though his eyes and nostrils show him that they are clean and fragrant.

In these cases, there is a condition for the attainment of knowledge that is not being fulfilled, and that has nothing to do with the means of knowledge involved, because the eyes of the person with the disorder described are functioning perfectly well.

The missing condition is faith, shraddha, without which knowledge does not occur. Or would anyone be willing to say that that person knows that his hands are clean? He doesn't know, because if he did, he would turn off the tap. That's all she wants.

To self-knowledge, being only a particular kind of knowledge, the same necessity applies: faith is required in the medium of knowledge which produces it.

And what is the medium of knowledge that produces it? It is called Veda, or, more precisely, Vedanta. Without faith that the words of Vedanta are a valid means of knowledge, it is not possible to gain the knowledge they are intended to reveal.

Without faith it is possible to get the information of what the words are saying, and it is even possible to become a Vedanta expert who gives lectures all over the world.

But such a person will talk about it in the following way: "According to Advaita Vedanta, the self (atma) is the whole (Brahman)." And in the same way he will say, for example, that according to Vishishta Advaita Vedanta the self is only a part of the whole, and so on.

Vedanta thus becomes, for sheer want of shraddha, just another theory, a system, and not a means of knowledge. All of us with some time of involvement with Vedanta know someone – usually from academia – who has been studying the subject for decades and probably knows more about the minutiae of the subject than we do, and yet cannot claim with conviction that it is already free, which, ironically, is all she wanted. The resemblance of this person to the OCD sufferer is no coincidence: they both suffer from the same lack of faith.

For this person, there is no point in studying more texts; It needs the previous qualification for the study of the texts, called faith, shraddha. In a famous text of the tradition called Vivekachudamani of Shankaracharya there is, in the section that talks about the qualification of the student, a very beautiful definition of faith that corroborates what we have been saying so far:

> *"Shastrasya guru-vakyasya satya-buddhi-avadharana sa shraddha kathita sadbhih yaya vastu-upalabhyate – the conviction that the words of the guru and the scripture are true is called faith by the sage, through which the truth is understood."*

The definition is quite bold: yaya vastu-upalabhyate means that the attainment of knowledge is because of the presence of shraddha, and without it there is no possibility of knowledge. This means that, in the case of Vedanta, the academic attitude of "convince me" born of the "neutrality" expected of a scientist prevents knowledge from establishing itself, leaving the scholar with only a full head and a sharp tongue.

And the interesting thing here is to note that the so-called academic neutrality, which supposedly prevents the academic from being previously committed, is just a farce, because being "neutral" is just a peculiar way of already being committed. And that is why mumukshutva, commitment to liberation is another prior qualification required for the study of Vedanta.

For any other compromise will hinder the faith necessary for knowledge to happen and fulfill its purpose of turning off the tap—stopping one's relentless pursuit of happiness or fulfillment.

5.3 Life is a school.

There are those who say that Life is a school. We go through it always learning something that increases our knowledge and our wisdom.

But are we aware of how this process occurs?

In his book *Metamanagement* (Antakarana Cultura Arte Ciência Ltda – SP), Fredy Kofman teaches, in a succinct but complete and profound way, how our learning occurs, and whose summary I describe below.

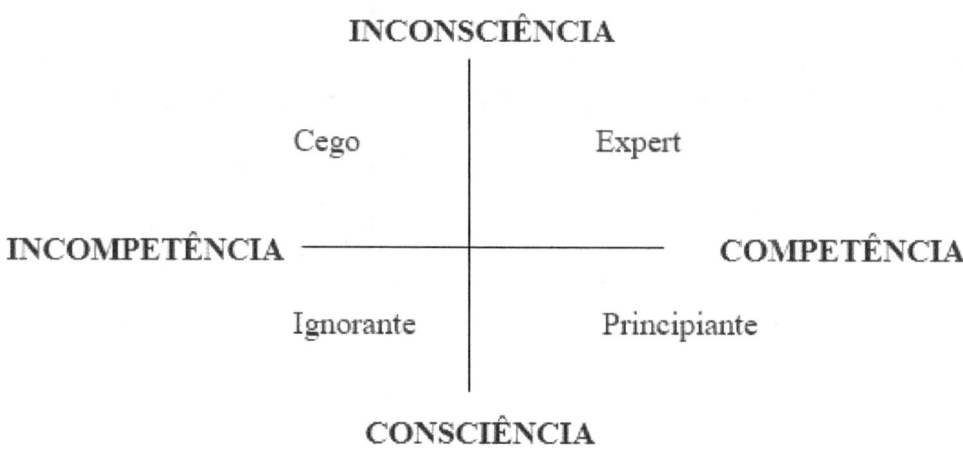

Figure 46 - The learning process.

Initially, it traces two axes: a vertical one (Unconsciousness – Consciousness) and a horizontal one (Incompetence – Competence), which intersect forming four quadrants that must be traversed in a counterclockwise direction.

In the upper left quadrant is the "blind" one. He is the one who, in addition to not knowing how to do it, does not even know that he does not know. Is unable to perform a given job or task. He is incompetent and unconscious. It usually frustrates and exasperates all those who have to deal with it.

By becoming conscious, the "blind" becomes an "ignorant", that is, while the former does not know that he does not know, the latter is aware of his incompetence.

At this point, the "ignorant" can take three paths:

1. Becoming an "absentee" and ignoring (abandoning) their field of action. This means that, aware of his incompetence, he will hire a person to carry out the task and remain on the sidelines. The "absent" does not generate competence, but prevents the persistence of errors:
2. Turning into a "cretin", that is, staying in the field of action, knowing that you don't know, but pretending to know. Aware of his own incapacity, he insists on not asking for help from an "expert";

3. Become a "beginner", that is, commit to learning and increasing effectiveness. You are always willing to learn, which generates commitment on your part. The "beginner" identifies his field of action and admits, without feeling ashamed, that he cannot be effective in accomplishing the task.

The "beginner" is required to complete four steps which, if not completed, will not characterize the "beginner", but a "cretin" who appears to be a "beginner". They are:

- Take responsibility for increasing their competence;
- Recognize yourself as a "beginner" and allow yourself to make mistakes;
- Seek help from a master or *coach* and give them permission and authority to help you;
- Dedicate the time and resources necessary to diligently practice what is being learned, always under the supervision of the master or *coach*, in a suitable space for it.

From then on, with his continuous learning, the "beginner" becomes an "expert", that is, he becomes consciously competent, skillful, knowing what has to be done and, based on his experiences, accomplishing what he considers to be the best at that moment. It reaches the upper right quadrant of the chart.

Congratulations!!! But..., is that all?

No, because the "expert" can become a "specialized incompetent," one who, having attained competence, ignores the changes taking place in his field of action. He does not change his way of acting, he is "frozen in time" and ends up becoming an ineffective person. The "expert," if he is not aware of the limitations of his ability, soon becomes obsolete.

So, which way? Becoming a "master" is the last stage of learning. It is the stage in which one achieves such a suitability that allows it to set new standards of excellence in the performance of tasks.

And what's the secret?

To maintain the spirit of "beginners", open and attentive to new creative possibilities that escape the "expert" in his unconscious competence. It's always having a desire to learn. The "master" is an eternal learner of knowledge. Like Socrates, a "master", he said: "The more I know, the more I know that I know nothing".

This is the script that makes us understand why some are more competent than others and why only a few can be called "masters".

5.4 CAVE MYTH.

Myth of the Cave or Allegory of the Cave is a Platonic dialogue that alludes to the preponderance of rational knowledge over vulgar knowledge.

The Myth of the Cave or Allegory of the Cave is a story narrated by Plato in his work The Republic. It is a dialogue between Glaucus and Socrates, in which Socrates tells a story to Glaucus to tell him about human knowledge.

5.4.1 What does the Myth of the Cave say?

Socrates tells Glaucus to imagine a kind of subterranean cave in which men have lived as prisoners forever. This cave has a wall in which the prisoners have been chained by the arms, so that they can only see what is going on in the parallel wall.

Figure 47 - The Myth of the Cave, or Allegory of the Cave.

Behind the prisoners, there is a burning flame through which people pass, gesticulate and move objects, so as to cast their shadows on the wall that the prisoners can see.

They also talk and shout, creating echoes that prisoners can hear. Shadows and echoes are distorted projections of real images and sounds. Because they live their entire lives there, in chains, all the prisoners know about the world is what they have experienced.

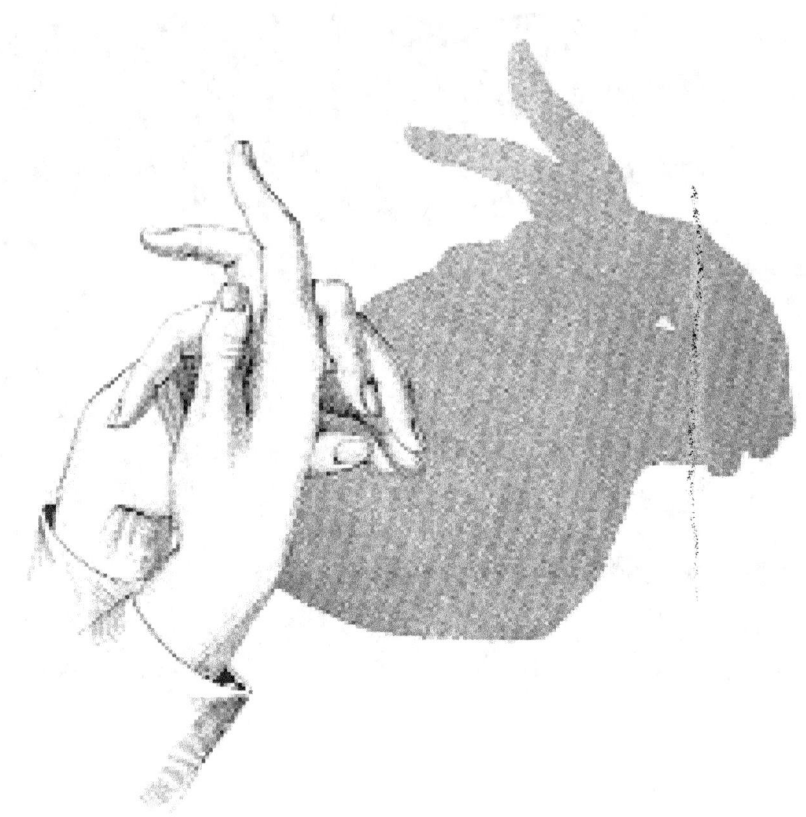

Figure 48 – A shadow on the wall.

Socrates tells Glaucus to imagine that one day a prisoner has been freed. He came out of the cave, had a first contact with sunlight that obscured his vision and generated a great nuisance. However, after becoming accustomed to the light, he was able to observe all of nature and the vast world outside the cave, much larger than he thought existed when he was a prisoner.

On a first impulse, the freed prisoner could try to return to the cave and free his companions. Imagining the possibilities, he could even be killed by his colleagues, who would judge him as crazy.

This metaphor is used by Plato to explain the hierarchy of knowledge and how this hierarchy is related to the politics of the city.

Figure 49- Plato is one of the thinkers of Ancient Greece.

5.4.2 Interpretation of the Cave Myth

The Allegory of the Cave is a metaphor, or as its name implies, an allegory. What is written in the text should not be taken literally, because Plato did not just want to tell a story about men trapped in a cave, but he wanted to convey a message with it.

Numerous metaphorical elements appear in the allegory. The main elements are laid out below:

- Prisoners: The prisoners in the cave are ourselves, the ordinary citizens.
- Cave: it is our body, which according to Plato, would be a source of deception and doubt, because it deceives us in the way we apprehend the appearances of things, making us believe that these are the things themselves.
- Shadows and echoes: the shadows that prisoners see and the echoes they hear are the opinions and prejudices that we bring from common

sense and customary life. They are, according to Plato, erroneous knowledge that we acquire through the senses of our body and everyday life.
- Coming out of the cave: The release of the prisoner and his escape from the cave symbolizes the search for true knowledge.
- The light of the sun: The sunlight outside the cave symbolizes true knowledge, reason, and philosophy. When the prisoner comes out of the cave, he is disturbed by the intense light, a natural element that he has never experienced before. At first, there is a difficulty in accepting this light by the retinas, until it adapts and perceives all external reality. Metaphorically, this symbolizes the comfort zone that the shadows and the cave represent, for the deception of ordinary life can be comfortable, while the truth can be, at least initially, painful and sacrificial. Getting out of ignorance means getting out of your comfort zone.

5.4.3 How would the Myth of the Cave fit in today?

People have a lot of information via television and the internet, but they remain at the level of information, not seeking to know things deeply.

We can transpose Platonic writings into a sociological interpretation of 21st-century humanity. Mankind seems to have become so accustomed to ignorance that there is a general refusal to seek truth.

People have an ocean of information through television media, the internet and social networks, but they remain at the merely informative level, not seeking to know deeply the world they inhabit.

Politics is no longer a matter of interest to the population. When the population seems to be interested in politics, it does so in a superficial way, without seeking to understand the essence of what is in focus. People are easily deceived and deceived by fake news spread on the internet because they don't bother to investigate whether what has been disseminated is real.

People believe the sensationalist headlines of news outlets that often aim only to get the reader's/viewer's attention, without reading the full content that the story brings.

Figure 50 – Too much access, too little knowledge.

The search for incessant pleasure, hedonism, the false idea of happiness, and vanity are values that people seek to pass on through social networks, but the intellectual content of these people is often limited to a very low level.

Knowledge, truth, goodness and justice are no longer sought after by the people of the 21st century, which is increasingly burying our society in ignorance and making us prisoners of our cave, like the prisoners of the Platonic allegory.

As Socrates supposed, near the end of the dialogue with Glaucus, the freed prisoner could be beaten or even killed while trying to rescue his companions, who would judge him as a madman, madman, for going against everything they had learned to be right.

In our days, there seems to be a similar movement, because the brilliant minds, the people who seek the deep knowledge of the causes, the scientists, the philosophers, are more and more challenged by people without any scientific or philosophical knowledge or basis, who use vulgar opinion to subjugate the value of science.

The predominance of shallow opinion, religious fanaticism and extremism has given way to the knowledge obtained during years of rational evolution of humanity. We are returning, of our own volition, to Plato's cave.

5.4.4 The Republic, the book containing the Myth of the Cave

The Republic is a work by Plato, divided into ten books, whose central theme is the political organization of the city. Considered a political utopia, Plato describes the numerous issues that should guide politics, including themes such as aesthetics and the theory of knowledge. The Myth of the Cave appears in Book VII of The Republic.

Socrates is the main character of the work, constructed in the form of dialogue. Throughout the text, there are interlocutors of Socrates who have an almost figurative function in the Platonic narrative.

The purpose of Book VII is to talk about knowledge, about the idea of justice (which is achieved by someone who possesses knowledge) and about the education of philosophers, who would be, in Platonic theory, the only ones to attain the knowledge necessary to govern the city well.

HUMAN CAPITAL AT WORK

"By viewing employees as a strategic asset and investing in their development, organizations are strengthening their human capital and increasing productivity, quality of work, and employee satisfaction."

Society for Human Resource Management (SHRM)

6 FAKE NEWS OR HOW TO DEVALUE THE IMPORTANCE OF EXPERIENCE.

The dissemination of fake news can negatively interfere with various sectors of society, such as politics, health, and security.

Figure 51 - Fake news is shared, mainly, on social networks.

Although it seems recent, the term fake news, or fake news, in Portuguese, is older than it seems. According to the Merriam-Webster dictionary, this expression has been used since the end of the nineteenth century. The term is in English, but it has become popular around the world to designate false information that is published, mainly, on social networks.

6.1 What does fake news mean?

It is not new that lies are disseminated as truths, but it was with the advent of social networks that this type of publication became popular. The international press began to use the term fake news more frequently during the 2016 election in the United States, in which Donald Trump became president. Fake news is an English term and is used to refer to false information disseminated, mainly, on social networks.

Around the time Trump was elected, some specialized companies identified a number of websites with dubious content. Most of the news published by these sites exploited sensationalist content, involving, in some cases, important personalities, such as Trump's opponent, Hillary Clinton.

6.2 How does fake news work?

The reasons for the creation of fake news are diverse. In some cases, the authors create absurd headlines with the clear intention of attracting access to the sites and, thus, making money from digital advertising.

However, beyond the purely commercial purpose, fake news can be used only to create rumors and reinforce a thought, through lies and the dissemination of hatred. In this way, ordinary people, celebrities, politicians and companies are harmed.

This is what happens, for example, during election periods, in which specialized companies create rumors, which are disseminated on a large scale on the network, reaching millions of users. The U.S. Department of Justice has indicted three Russian agencies, saying they spread false information on the internet and influenced the 2016 U.S. election.

There are specific groups that work by spreading rumors. However, it is not easy to find companies that operate in this segment, as they operate on the so-called deep web, that is, a part of the network that is not indexed by search engines, being hidden from the general public.

Figure 52 - Fake news hackers usually operate in a zone of the internet called the deep web.

Fake news hackers usually operate in a zone of the internet called the deep web.

To disseminate false information, a website is created. A robot created by the programmers of these groups is responsible for disseminating the link on the networks. The more the subject is mentioned on the networks, the more the robot acts, even firing information every two seconds, which is humanly impossible.

With such a volume of content dissemination, real people are vulnerable to fake news and end up sharing this information. In this way, a network of lies with real people is created.

As those responsible for fake news usually operate in a region of the web that is hidden from the vast majority of users, it is not easy to identify them and, consequently, punish them. In addition, these people use servers from outside the country, in lan houses that do not require identification.

6.3 Examples and consequences of fake news

Any kind of false information, from the simplest to the most misplaced, misleads people. In many cases, the news contains false information surrounded by true information. It is mainly in these situations that the dangers of fake news are hidden, and its consequences can be disastrous.

One case that became known and reached the extreme was that of housewife Fabiane Maria de Jesus, who died after being beaten by dozens of residents of Guarujá, on the coast of São Paulo, in 2014. The residents' revolt was due to information published on a social network, with a spoken portrait of a possible kidnapper of children for black magic rituals. The housewife was mistaken for the criminal and ended up lynched by residents.

Another rumor that took over the networks and directly influenced the childhood vaccination schedule was that some vaccines would be deadly and would have killed thousands of children. The impact was so great that diseases such as measles, from which Brazil was considered free, once again affected children.

After the truckers' strike in 2018, which lasted 11 days, closed highways from north to south of the country and caused shortages of various products, some rumors of a new strike generated turmoil in large cities. In some municipalities, lines of cars formed at gas stations, as people feared the increase in price and even the lack of the product.

At election time, it is common for candidates or voters to use lies to gain an advantage. With so many voters on social media, a well-planted lie can alter the course of an election, as in the case of the 2016 elections in the United States.

A serious fact that was found by researchers from the Massachusetts Institute of Technology (MIT), in the United States, is that the chance of fake news being passed on is considerably greater than that of a real one. A total of 126,000 news items were analyzed, and it was found that the probability of republishing false information is 70% higher than that of republishing true news.

Figure 53 - The chances of fake news being passed on are much higher than those of true news.

6.4 How to fight fake news?

For the authorities, identifying and punishing the authors of rumors on the network is a very difficult task. In the case of Brazil, the legislation that provides punishment for this type of crime does not talk about the internet, it only mentions radio and television.

Some fake news sites use addresses and layouts similar to those of major news portals, inducing Internet users to think that they are credible pages. That's why you can't be too careful on the internet.

The most effective way to reduce the impacts of fake news is for each citizen to do their part, sharing only what they are sure is true. The ideal is to always doubt and look for information in other vehicles, especially in the so-called mainstream media.

In Brazil, there are agencies that specialize in checking the veracity of suspicious news and rumors, the so-called fact-checking. Some major news portals have also created sectors for fact-checking.

Here are some fact-checking pages in Brazil:

- Magnifying Glass Agency
- To the Facts
- Truco
- UOL Confers
- Boatos.org
- E-scams

6.5 False science can be fatal.

It is important to seek the truth of the facts in order to have a reliable knowledge base. Ignorance of the truth, or knowledge that is not put into practice, can be fatal. This basic principle applies at levels from staff to planetarium.

Falsification affects science as well as everyday social information, and once the two have become highly interactive globally, a vicious cycle operates dangerously on an increasing scale.

The fake news/fake science cycle undermines the credibility of science and the ability of individuals and society to make evidence-informed choices in their best interest.

At the individual level, a lack of reliable knowledge about how to maintain physical, nutritional, and personal health safety can result in avoidable harm or death.

One example is the childhood illnesses, permanent disabilities, and deaths that have resulted worldwide from the fabricated scientific report that the measles, mumps, and rubella (MMR) vaccine causes autism.

Despite the proven record of efficacy of vaccines in preventing infections from deadly diseases, the widespread spread of this lie, especially through social media, resulted not only in record levels of measles infections in Europe in 2018, but also fueled a growing, broader phenomenon known as 'vaccine hesitancy'.

On a collective level, false information can alter attitudes and policies on crucial ecological, social, and political issues, and at the extreme, it can put entire populations at national, regional, and even global levels at risk of harm.

For example, the denial of anthropogenic climate change, dismissed without counter-evidence as 'fake science', has resulted in the loss of universal acceptance of the international agreement on climate change and its impact on the level of global warming is likely to have disastrous consequences worldwide in the 21st century.

The depiction of ethnic groups, foreigners, or foreign states as enemies through false stories is an ancient technique that has gained new potency through modern methods of mass communication and can provoke genocides and wars.

Fake Twitter accounts were used to send millions of messages aimed at influencing attitudes towards Brexit in the 2016 UK referendum and opinions on candidates in the 2016 US presidential election.

6.6 Validated information needs to be put into practice.

Awareness of the evidence that smoking causes serious illness and that tobacco kills up to half of its users has not yet allowed 1.1 billion smokers worldwide to kick their habit or governments to introduce outright bans on smoking.

Denial, fake news, the deliberate weakening of true data by portraying it as "junk science" to distort public health policies, fabricated information, distortion of the media framing, and secret illicit trade have all been documented in the decades-long battle of the tobacco industry and its adherents to sustain their lucrative but fatal trade.

Examples such as climate change and tobacco illustrate the difficulties that both individuals and society can have in determining what is factually correct, how to recognize the biases and vested interests that may underlie the information available, and how to balance risks and benefits at personal, national, and global levels.

6.7 Evolution of scientific validation.

A critical factor is the question of who has the authority to determine the reliability of the facts and judge the veracity of the information offered.

Since ancient times, those with wealth, power, and high hierarchical positions were treated as privileged sources, as were some individuals regarded as altruistic seekers of wisdom in the realms of spirituality, scholarship, or science.

Since its introduction by Francis Bacon (1561-1626), the evolved scientific method has included unbiased observations that are evaluated for reproducibility and subjected to careful self-criticism and logical thinking about their meaning and implications, then offered for inspection by the world at large.

The establishment of scholarly societies and the publication of periodicals, beginning with the Philosophical Transactions of the Royal Society, first published in 1665, provided a mechanism for presenting information that could be critically examined by the scientific community.

If refuted, the prevailing models and theories would be replaced by new ones, more consistent with the state of contemporary knowledge. This provisional character of science is not a weakness, but one of the main reasons for its strength.

The evolution of this process, in the second half of the twentieth century, established a 'gold standard' for the reliability of knowledge. It has been the basis of the esteem in which science has been held, as an honest and unbiased source of evidence-based knowledge, not only to advance the frontiers of the field, but also to inform the public and politicians and assist in decision-making.

Richard Burdon Haldane's landmark 1918 report to the British Prime Minister signalled the strength of the evolving relationship between science and politics, with Haldane championing the principle that politicians should stay out of decisions about research funding, listen to experts, have time to think and reflect before coming to a conclusion, and, When asking scientists for advice, resist telling them what that advice should be.

6.8 The changing scenario: the revolution in the production of knowledge.

While the degree of importance of scientific contributions to policymaking continues to be debated, the current revolution in knowledge production has further complicated the issue.

An illustration of the extent to which the landscape has changed was seen in the centennial year of the 'Haldane Principle', which witnessed a major scientific report commissioned by the US government and issued by 13 federal agencies – warning of the consequences of climate change and therefore at odds with government policies – being rejected by several leading politicians, including the president, on the grounds that they 'don't believe it', while they (baselessly) accused climate scientists of being driven by money.

In 1991, Harnad described four stages in the means of knowledge production in human beings. The first three were the emergence of language (hundreds of thousands of years ago) and the invention of writing (several thousand years ago) and printing (more than 500 years ago).

The fourth had begun very recently, with the invention of the Internet and the ability it offers anyone in the world to be a publisher—to communicate any information they want, true or false, instantly and globally.

Facts and their denial are no longer determined by any kind of authority, but, in principle, by each individual, regardless of his or her education and reputation or knowledge of a carefully acquired field.

Manipulation of data by anyone (including scientists) becomes easier and easier. Due to the ready availability of information and communication technology (ICT) tools and access to the Internet and social media, there are today numerous ways to create and distribute products of unknown veracity, including manipulated textual and pictorial material. Anarchist philosopher of science Paul Feyerabend's predictions that 'anything goes' and conceptual artist Joseph Beuys that 'every human being is an artist' have thus come true.

In his 1943 essay on the Spanish Civil War, writer George Orwell acknowledged the way people in politics and wars make use of available propaganda mechanisms to create their own versions of truth, expressing his fear that 'the very concept of objective truth is disappearing from the world'.

This ongoing challenge has been exacerbated and greatly accelerated by ICTs and the fourth revolution in knowledge production. As Harnad acknowledged, each of these knowledge revolutions represented a profound and qualitative change in both HOW human beings communicate and think and WHAT is thought.

6.9 Consequences for science and for scientific publication and evaluation

The impacts of the fourth revolution, barely seen three decades ago, are now dramatically evident, even in contemporary language. One sign was Ralph Keyes's 2004 statement that "we live in a post-truth era" – a stage of social evolution that is "beyond honesty" in which "deception has become commonplace at all levels of contemporary life".

More recent signs were the emergence in 2017 of the term 'alternative facts' to describe inaccurate data and the designation of 'truth is not true' as the 2018 Citation of the Year.

There are increasing impacts both at the interface between science and society and in the domain of science itself. It has been argued that in the current political and media environment, 'distrust of the scientific enterprise and misperceptions of scientific knowledge stem increasingly... the wide dissemination of misleading and biased information'.

The philosopher Bruno Latour observed that "facts remain robust only when they are supported by a common culture, by reliable institutions, by a more or less decent public life, by a more or less reliable media."

While research into the public's view of the trustworthiness of scientists yields results that vary with time and place, in his 2017 book on the 'death of expertise', Tom Nichols described the many forces trying to undermine the authority of 'experts', so that the term itself began to be used contemptuously to justify the rejection of their advice.

In the face of this challenge, it is especially important for the scientific world as a whole to maintain the highest standards of ethical behavior, honesty, and transparency, in order to maintain gold standards of research integrity and validated information. Unfortunately, a number of forces are working against this aspiration.

> *People in the world of science are not immune to the personal ambitions and prevailing pressures that drive behavior in general.*

As recently described, three closely related subsystems (science advancement, reputation rewards, and financial returns) collectively form an overall system of scientific publishing that has become heavily flawed.

Encourages scientists to distort and exaggerate their results in the pursuit of new grants, promotions, and distinctions; and it encourages editors to cherry-pick the work, exaggerate the results, and distort the arbitration in the competition for high status and correspondingly high profits from publication fees.

Both authors and editors are encouraged to play the system to mutual benefit. At the extreme, the perverse incentives generated result in authors fabricating data, predatory journals hunting for articles, and the creation of fake journals that seek only the authors' fees for processing the articles.

The scale of the problem of fake science is becoming more and more evident. The percentage of scientific papers retracted for fraud has increased by an order of magnitude since 2000 and high retraction rates are observed for the most prestigious journals, illustrating both the extent to which flawed claims are perpetrated by scientists seeking prominence and weaknesses and even falsification in the current practice of peer review. A recent investigation of publishing in predatory 'open access' journals and fake conferences has revealed a global ecosystem of predatory publishers churning out 'fake science' for profit.

The intrusion of such journals into the traditionally respected space of scientific publishing seriously undermines the integrity and credibility of science and, if not stopped and sanctioned immediately, could become fatal to the field as we know it.

It is a fundamental strength of the scientific system that incorrect knowledge will eventually be discovered and discarded. However, the pace and scale at which material that is at best dubious and at worst deliberately false is being published is now creating a crisis.

The consequences are very detrimental to the scientific enterprise, with a loss of respect for the results of science and the scientific method, leading, among others, to a sharp decline in funding, jobs, and students wishing to enter the field.

The crisis is also hurting society, creating an 'anything goes' environment in which 'alternative facts' go untested and decisions that affect the lives of people everywhere are not informed by authentic data or valid conclusions. Thus, in the new era of the fourth revolution in the means of knowledge production.

6.10 Ways forward

Fake science and fake news are complex phenomena that involve a variety of causes, dissemination channels, and consequences. Solving the challenges they pose will not be achieved by a single approach or simple set of measures, but will require a concerted effort from a wide range of actors across sectors.

To address the overall societal problem of fake news, several initiatives underway or under discussion offer promising approaches. In addition to those that directly involve science and scientists, which are discussed separately below, they include the following.

Efforts are needed to combat the spread of false information via social media, through modifications to computer algorithms that favor the 'bias' of stories with no factual basis, and the development of tools that help identify and develop skills in recognizing false claims.

The limitations of large-scale automated approaches and the ingenuity with which they can be manipulated must, however, be acknowledged.

There should be more efforts to increase the responsibility taken by social media services for the content they allow online. The fundamental question of whether social media should be regarded as 'platforms' that are not responsible for content (as social media maintains) or as 'publishers' that can, like traditional print publishers, be held accountable for the content they disseminate (as some critics of the current position propose), with many legal, regulatory, financial, ethical and operational ramifications, remains in dispute.

Meanwhile, there has been widespread dissatisfaction with the results of social media self-regulation to date, and highly publicized failures in areas such as politics, racism, and health have led to calls for more regulation and/or more action through social media. Necessary initiatives include efforts to increase the speed and scope of measures to remove offensive and harmful materials and to develop algorithms to detect and exclude fraudulent sources.

Scientists should not remain bystanders in the battle against falsehood in the news in general, as well as in their own domains of expertise.

They can contribute to the understanding of the phenomenon of fake news, which has usually been studied along four lines: characterization, creation, circulation, and combat.

A multidisciplinary effort is needed to better understand how the internet spreads content and how readers process the news and information they consume, as well as how social media platforms are manipulated to amplify particular stories through the use of fake accounts and 'bots'. As an example, WhatsApp has selected 20 research teams around the world, including from India, to work to understand how misinformation spreads and what additional steps the mobile messaging platform can take to curb fake news.

Scientists must be willing to speak up when they see false information being presented on social media, traditional print media, or broadcast press.

They should use these means fully themselves to offer facts and evidence in succinct layman's language, emphasizing the breadth and depth of the scientific consensus that underpins the current state of knowledge and pointing to the lack of scientific rigor in false information.

They must be willing to contradict public leaders and opinion makers who condemn or reject valid science without offering verified evidence of their own, as has happened, for example, in the US and India.

In the long run, scientists must be better advocates and contributors to the generation of a more scientifically literate society. The ultimate defense against false facts is the ability of each individual to critically examine the information offered and come to a judgment about its reliability based on evidence and reasoning.

Scientists can contribute to inculcating the 'scientific temperament' in society. This term, coined in 1946 by Jawaharlal Nehru, describes a way of life, a process of thinking and acting that utilizes the scientific method and may consequently include questioning, observing, testing, hypothesizing, analyzing, and communicating.

The role of journalism remains important, and the development by scientists of stronger links with reputable journalists can encourage clearer and more accurate research reporting.

In the realm of science itself, individually and collectively through their professional associations, academic institutions, and funding agencies, scientists must act to put their own house in order, promoting ethical practices and research integrity, dealing with the problems of reproducibility and retractions, developing policies and practices to discourage the production and publication of false data and results, and the use of 'predatory' peer-reviewed journals and making maximum use of emerging artificial intelligence capabilities to detect and expose falsified data and images.

Examples where measures are already being adopted or explored include India's use of a 'white list' to discourage researchers from publishing in predatory journals.

Education – both broadly as part of life skills development and specifically in the culture and methods of science – is an essential part of the long-term solution, so that young people are equipped with the knowledge, skills and tools to be able to critically examine information and assess its veracity.

As noted by the President of the European Research Council, 'We need to form a new generation of critical minds. Science is not about learning long-established facts of color; it's knowing how to question and move on.

Most young people rely primarily on social media to get their news, so we must deal with this issue through better news literacy, and it is the task of our educators and society at large to teach children how to use doubt intelligently and understand that uncertainty can be quantified and measured.

Research indicates that preemptively inoculating people before they receive misinformation (pre-bunking) is more effective than refuting after receipt (debunking) in reducing the influence of misinformation. Synthesizing separate lines of research from education, cognitive psychology, and inoculation theory (a branch of psychological research) provides a coherent set of recommendations for educators and communicators.

Scientific explanations that involve the clear communication of scientific concepts and the current scientific consensus are ideally combined with inoculating explanations of how that science can be distorted.

6.11 What is the role of a leader in stopping fake news in the workplace?

Misinformation comes in many shapes and sizes, and it affects your business as well. Everything from sharing fake news to spreading rumors can spell trouble, especially among larger collectives.

Letting these things run wild risks erodes trust in the company, creates conflicts among employees, impacts productivity, and leads to costly misunderstandings. For example, an unhealthy work environment can lead good workers to look for other opportunities.

It's increasingly important for leaders to moderate the company's discussion channels and settings to avoid the negative impacts of nonsense. That's not to say you have to play the role of thought policeman, tell people what to think, or meddle in every employee discussion. Doing so will likely only serve to further aggravate the situation.

Instead, the manager's primary role in stopping the spread of fake news in the company is to equip their team with the tools, resources, and know-how to be able to evaluate the things they share and discuss on the company's channels. Particularly when it comes to communication about the company. And only interfere when absolutely necessary.

6.12 What is misinformation in the workplace and how to identify it?

While there's certainly something to be said for our collective responsibility to stop fake news in general, managers can't be the sole arbiters of truth and check everything that's shared.

Additionally, misinformation in the workplace can include rumors, clickbait, conspiracy theories, and outright lies, and even the best-trained leaders and employees are susceptible to falling victim to credible information.

Thus, the kind of misinformation that should be scrutinized in the company is harmful office gossip and inflammatory news — the things that are most likely to contribute to office toxicity.

Figure 54 – Fake news can cause suffering in teams.

Understanding what qualifies as inflammatory is a challenge in itself, however, knowing your team's backgrounds and getting to know them as you work together can go a long way in helping you understand where they stand. Also, as a rule of thumb, it's best to leave hotbutton issues untouched unless it's absolutely clear that everyone is on the same page.

6.13 6 Ways to Stop Fake News in the Workplace.

It's up to the company's leadership to lay the groundwork for a healthy office information space. Let's look at 3 ways on how this can be achieved.

1. Foster a culture of transparency.

    Fight bad communication with good communication. Office rumors and misinformation about the company often sprout when there is an information vacuum. The answer is self-evident – don't let that vacuum exist.

    Continuous updates and interaction from superiors who provide the company's official position and views on social, corporate, and financial topics can curb the spread of inaccurate information and align everyone.

    Openly discussing the good, the bad, and the ugly demonstrates trust in the team and encourages public discussions that don't allow resentment to fester in the shadows. Of course, communication needs to be two-way and give the team a means through which they can express themselves.

    With tools like SpeakUp – an anonymous message board for businesses – even the shyest employees can make themselves heard without fear of repercussions.

    Openness in company-related discussions can also have a knock-on effect on non-work-related conversations, as people learn to communicate transparently and without hostility.

2. Educate staff on how to spot fake news.

    We'll say it again, but it's worth repeating – the manager shouldn't be an arbiter of truth. Teaching employees how to critically evaluate information is the best thing you can do to stop fake news from spreading in the workplace and take some of the weight off the manager's shoulders.

From conducting a critical thinking workshop to disseminating information on tactics to verify the accuracy of content, education is one of the strongest tools in your arsenal. And the managers who oversee their team need to be proficient in these things.

When you find possible misinformation in the company, you should:

- Verify its veracity – read the information, check its sources, examine the author, and check with other sources.
- Examine your biases – familiarize yourself with some of the most common critical thinking mistakes and make sure you don't fall victim to them, e.g., confirmation bias, availability bias, anchoring bias, etc.
- Be mindful of who is sharing. Understanding where the news is coming from can go a long way in telling you how to respond diplomatically.

If everyone on your team understands the basics of information analysis, you'll not only slow down fake news, but you'll also gain a more competent team.

3. Lead by example.

Knowing how to identify misinformation is not enough. Things often seem believable both on the surface and upon further investigation, so it's almost inevitable that some things will slip through.

Do not hesitate to change your mind frequently and publicly when you become aware of new facts. Even if it's about some discussion that took place months earlier, revisiting it and explaining what has changed (e.g., you've lost faith in the source) can go a long way in changing the opinion of your colleagues who still accept the previous version of the facts.

In addition, it will demonstrate how to use the second most important tool in combating misinformation – changing your mind. The goal, after all, is not the exercise of detecting fake news. The goal is to believe true things.

4. Encourage your employees to consult verified sources of information.

    While for some people it's hard to believe fake news, the reality is that not everyone bothers to check whether something they've read is true or not. Encourage your employees to consult local government health information or check for up-to-date information on official websites such as OSHA and CDC.

5. Build fluent and transparent communication

    Make sure you have the right communication channels in place to inform your employees and communicate with them frequently. Additionally, regular and transparent communication will give you more visibility into what employees are most concerned about or need to clarify. By doing so, you can solve your queries on a daily basis or share regular updates.

6. Put safety first

    Security is not a choice. Remember that employers have a responsibility to determine workplace safety best practices. For this reason, it is important for leaders to be able to build a strong workplace safety culture to promote particular behaviors and attitudes among employees. Demonstrate to employees that their safety is more important than any dubious information. As one security professional put it, "Regardless of what your personal opinions are, it's better to be safe than sorry."

For managers, fighting misinformation means walking a fine line – you must hone in on the company's pitch without overextending it. Still, it's a productive endeavor that can improve office dynamics by creating a more welcoming environment for employees and promoting better communication between them.

At the end of the day, the most valuable activity is education. Nip fake news in the workplace in the bud by teaching people to recognize and avoid sharing misinformation will allow managers to spend less time fighting fires and more time focusing on value-added activities.

That said, as we move into a post-truth era, divisions in opinion are likely to become more pronounced and increasingly trickle down to our workplaces. Targeted action is necessary to ensure that it doesn't become a problem in your company.

In these times of fighting fake news, it is even more difficult to defend the value of experience. It seems that everything that sustains the world is in constant check.

HUMAN CAPITAL AT WORK

"Valuing human capital at work is not just about offering competitive wages, but also about fostering an environment where people feel recognized, inspired, and empowered to reach their full potential."

World Economic Forum

7 SOFT SKILLS: WHAT THEY ARE, EXAMPLES AND HOW TO DEVELOP.

Soft skills are behavioral skills related to the way the professional deals with others and with himself in different situations. Soft skills, unlike hard skills, are subjective skills that are more difficult to measure.

Have you ever heard of soft skills? The term refers to skills related to a professional's personality, such as communication skills or teamwork.

Figure 55 – Soft Skills.

According to a study by recruitment website CareerBuilder[3], 77% of companies believe that soft skills are as important as technical skills in their day-to-day work.

---

[3] https://www.prnewswire.com/news-releases/overwhelming-majority-of-companies-say-soft-skills-are-just-as-important-as-hard-skills-according-to-a-new-careerbuilder-survey-254697151.html

7.1 What are soft skills?

The term soft skills usually goes hand in hand with hard skills, both of which are used by Human Resources professionals to identify specific characteristics of a professional.

Hard skills are technical skills and, in general, they are easily measurable and possible to develop through training and courses, for example. For a long time, this competence was the main and most relevant professionally, but this scenario has been transformed and currently soft skills appear with much more relevance and prominence.

Soft skills, on the other hand, refer to behavioral skills related to the way a person deals with others, that is, how their interaction in groups works and, at the same time, how they deal with their own emotions. The more positively the professional is able to deal with these environmental and psychological situations, the greater their soft skills.

However, despite the importance of soft skills, they are difficult to measure and develop, as they are subjective skills, therefore, they are closely related to personality and other emotional factors built throughout the individual's life.

With this in mind, it is possible to understand why soft skills are so valued today.

7.2 Exemplos de soft skills

1. Emotional Intelligence

Emotional intelligence is the ability to recognize and deal with one's own emotions and the emotions of others. Initially, it consists of identifying emotions through physiological aspects in order to later have a deeper understanding of a reaction, recognize non-evident emotions and, finally, deal with one's own feelings and the feelings of others.

2. Resilience

Resilience is closely related to the response given by the individual when faced with adverse situations or when having to make a decision under pressure. Generally speaking, it is the ability to deal with problems assertively and adapt easily.

3. Assertive communication

Communication is very important in different functions, however, depending on how it is done, it can incite or appease conflicts. At the same time, if the message is not comprehensible, there may be problems in understanding demands and, consequently, in processes and deliveries. So, to avoid conflicts and maintain linearity in the processes, it is important that there is assertive communication within the teams.

7.3 What are the soft skills most in demand by companies?

It is the soft skills that will indicate to the recruiter how the professional deals with the challenges of everyday life. According to the CareerBuilder survey, cited at the outset, the ten most sought-after soft skills by organizations are:

- Ethical principles;
- Confidence;
- Positive attitude;
- Motivation;
- Teamwork;
- Organization and time management;
- Ability to work under pressure;
- Communication;
- Flexibility;
- Safety.

1.1 What are the differences between soft skills and hard skills?

In addition to soft skills, so-called hard skills are also evaluated by recruiters. This category includes the candidate's technical skills, such as the ability to operate a machine, the level of proficiency in some software, or specific knowledge in a certain area of expertise.

The most important difference between soft skills and hard skills lies in learning. Technical skills can be acquired in college, in free courses, and in previous work experiences. Soft skills, on the other hand, are parts of the professional's personality, personal characteristics that he or she probably carries throughout his or her life.

Of course, soft skills can also be taught, trained, and developed, but this is a much more time-consuming process. Can you imagine how difficult it would be to turn an aggressive manager into a charismatic leader? Teaching a layman in audiovisual how to use a video editing tool would be much simpler.

7.4 What is the importance of soft skills?

There are many strategic advantages to hiring people who have developed soft skills. In order for the team to deliver the expected results, a good relationship between colleagues is essential. That's where communication and teamwork skills come in, for example. If the professionals on the team have these skills, it is easy to establish a productive and harmonious day-to-day.

Another situation in which soft skills are needed is in solving day-to-day problems. Proactive professionals often look for solutions on their own, bringing managers only issues that are completely out of their reach. When the team doesn't depend so much on leadership decisions, processes become dynamic and results happen faster and more efficiently.

The fact that this type of competency is a transferable skill is also a plus point. This means that, with daily interaction, the people on the team can gradually learn soft skills from each other.

A professional with an extremely positive attitude, for example, can transform the way the entire team thinks over time. However, the opposite also happens: a negative person, who only complains, can end up contaminating the environment. That's why it's important to worry about recruiting employees with the right profile.

Finally, it is important to note that soft skills can be used in any type of profession or job. That is, in the event that a financial analyst is transferred to the marketing area, he can be very successful if he is a creative and communicative person.

7.5   How to assess soft skills during the job interview?

Technical skills are easier to assess than soft skills. If a candidate states on their resume that their English is fluent, they just need to apply oral or written tests to prove whether the statement is true or not. This goes for software proficiency and other specific knowledge.

So, how can you assess soft skills effectively? For this, a special dedication is required at the time of the interview. Asking the right questions and paying attention to the answers is key to identifying if the candidate has the desired personal characteristics.

Ideally, the interviewee should know how to make the connection between their skills and professional results and have a naturally empathetic, optimistic and collaborative worldview.

There is no magic formula, of course, but we have listed some questions that can help in this mission. Check it out below!

"Tell me about a time when you had to work as a team."

If the candidate badmouths the group they worked for and says they needed to work everything out themselves, dismiss them. Even if the story is true, a good interviewee would tell it differently. An answer like this means that the person didn't prepare well for the interview, since they don't know that they shouldn't criticize their former colleagues.

The best answer, in this case, is one that describes how the contributions of everyone in the group were important to the success of the project. If the candidate can tell about his own work and still value the work of those who helped him, he can be sure that he is a professional with strong teamwork skills.

"Talk about a situation in which you needed to ask for help."

This is another good question to assess whether or not the candidate knows how to work in a team. If he says he doesn't remember, be suspicious. A professional who works well in a group knows that no one is good at everything and makes a point of asking for help from colleagues whenever necessary. And, of course, he is also always helpful in providing support to his companions. This type of employee will have no difficulty answering the question.

"If you ever had to perform a role that is outside of your job description, how would you react?"

This question evaluates the candidate's proactivity and versatility. Professionals without these soft skills will somehow make their discomfort with this type of situation evident, even if they try to disguise it. If the interviewee is truly willing and able to perform any type of function, point to him.

7.6   How to develop soft skills in your employees?

As we have seen, it is not difficult to identify soft skills in candidates for new positions in the organization. Now, we'll look at how to develop soft skills in talents that are already part of the organizational structure. It may seem like a big challenge, but with the right techniques, you can help employees develop their skills.

Some recommended techniques are:

1. Try to make employees aware of the importance of soft skills and how they can help them achieve more success, both at work and in their personal lives.

2. Provoke reflections on what new social skills could help them. For example: how can the ability to communicate assertively help a manager to get more participation and results from his team?
3. Invest in the development of soft skills, offering training with the aim of educating work teams. This is a good way to reinforce the organization's interest in the success of its employees and strengthen the organizational culture.
4. Identify each team member's pain points to provide personalized learning. It is also important not to overwhelm the professional and train one skill at a time, so that the process is efficient.
5. Show confidence and, as your employees develop, give them more responsibility. Show that you believe in their potential, and they will feel more stimulated to expose their ideas and be more proactive.
6. Prioritize teamwork, as collaborating toward common goals is an excellent way to develop and hone social skills.

Understand that developing soft skills is not something you can achieve quickly.

It may be necessary to reinforce training and always offer support and the necessary tools for them to stay on the path of development.

7.7 What tools can be used in the development of soft skills?

It is essential to invest in tools that help in the development of employees' soft skills. They can be applied both in the work environment and at a distance, covering every aspect of learning and making it more dynamic and efficient. Here are some options.

1. E-learning.

This distance learning tool allows employees to manage their learning time and have access to the best content from the best companies and institutions in the world, without having to travel long distances to do so.

In addition, the tool allows the use of videos, where learners can observe behaviors more attentively, being able to watch as many times as necessary to absorb their content.

2. Individual development plan.

With the individual development plan, it is possible to sign an agreement between manager and employee for the development of skills. The objective, means and goals are defined in advance, and the professional seeks to fulfill his steps and tasks while being monitored and evaluated by his superior.

7.8 Leadership. The main soft skill of the successful professional.

Leadership is a different characteristic, as there are many professionals who are successful and who do not have this competence and we cannot define it as a mandatory characteristic to be successful.

Many professionals, extremely talented at what they do, stand out for their professionalism and are respected for their work. But they don't have the characteristics of the leader. So why mention this characteristic here as being part of the profile of the professional in the modern world? It is because, although it is not mandatory to be successful, it will open up greater opportunities for success.

A leader stands out for always being ahead of the pack. People recognize the leader as being a booster for others. Decisions can be made together, but it is the leaders who will be at the forefront in carrying out the decisions made.

The leader knows how to motivate others. Because when he is at the head of the group, he manages to make the others surpass themselves.

In the face of the problems that arise, true leaders stand out, because when everyone is bewildered, the leader is able to see beyond the obvious, finding solutions in the inexplicable and very calmly directing people to the right side, often motivating them to find the solution to problems by themselves.

We have countless examples of people who possess a leadership attitude. Just look at one sport and you'll see that successful teams almost always have a leader who pushes the others to achieve results.

For the professional, leadership will bring benefits, because the leader is not only found in leadership positions, because even where only two people work if one of them is a leader, the goals tend to be easier to achieve.

Companies are looking for true leaders and not just bosses, managers, or directors. Being a boss is not synonymous with being a leader, because countless bosses, often admired for their high administrative competence, fail to create in their subordinates the necessary motivation for them to give their all. A successful company is not only made up of good directors, managers, or bosses, but also of great leaders.

But how does a leader act? The leader is certainly not that professional who stands still, watching everything happen around him without doing anything. No, the leader is participative, questions when necessary, supports the decisions made and is at the forefront of being an example to other professionals in the organization.

Unfortunately, there are leaders, often even with the innate characteristic, who instead of leading in favor of the good, end up using their leadership in favor of what is wrong, that is, they are those professionals who are the first to oppose the decisions made within the organization and even influencing other professionals to do the same.

And because we mention the verb "influence," this ability is one of the best characteristics of a true leader. He knows how to talk and convince, because talking, everyone knows from an early age, but having the ability to influence speech is quite different than simply talking. Let's break down what are the main characteristics of the leader:

- Influences people – The leader influences people positively so that they have the motivation to achieve their own goals as well as those of the organization they work for.

- He is empathetic – He knows how to put himself in the shoes of others, trying to understand those he leads and knowing how to adequately meet their needs, taking into account their education, age, education, gender, values and other factors.
- Listen to people – Take the time to listen to people, especially subordinates, rather than just listening to them selflessly. This is key to earning their respect.
- Counseling – The leader must be an advisor, able to continually steer the team in the "true north," i.e., the right direction.
- Demonstrate ideas clearly – It's not enough to have ideas if people don't know how to talk about them. The clarity in the placement of ideas makes it easier for them to be accepted. I have often noticed that when I talk to people one day, I see the next day that they had not understood anything I had said or had understood it in a way that was totally contrary to what I had said, so I try to make sure that people clearly understood what I was trying to express.
- It is flexible – It is important for the leader to be flexible, being able to review decision-making in favor of their team, or even in the face of new situations that arise.
- It has a systemic view – Systemic view means the view of the whole, knowing the entire process or system, even if not detailed, in order to understand the operation of the company.
- Know the market – Knowing the market as a whole, which includes competitors, suppliers, and customers, as well as keeping track of their respective trends is part of a leader's skills.
- Professionalism – Professionalism, as the name implies, is being professional, respecting people, treating them appropriately, being able to separate friendship and kinship from professional matters.
- Possesses skills to deal with adversity – The leader is able to remain calm and calm their subordinates in the face of the greatest adversity. When we are under pressure and high stress, we tend to make rash, thoughtless, and wrong decisions. In addition, when the leader gets

disoriented, his team loses its way. Therefore, it is very important to know how to deal with adversity.

It's up to you to assess the extent to which you possess the characteristics of a leader. This book won't cover all aspects of a leader, which might not even fit in a book, because we're actually talking about a set of skills that make up a great professional.

Think about yourself and see if it's worth improving your qualities to become a great leader. Some are leaders, but they haven't realized it yet, which may happen to you.

In case you've already convinced yourself of this, now is the time to continue to demonstrate that you're a true leader.

HUMAN CAPITAL AT WORK

"The value of human capital at work lies in people's ability to bring unique knowledge, skills, and experiences to organizations, driving innovation, collaboration, and growth."

Forbes

8   ANDRAGOGY – ADULT EDUCATION.

Of all the beings of nature, man is the only being conscious of the acts he does and the only one who has the capacity to increase his knowledge of his own free will. That's why it's the most developed of them all.

To say that the search for new knowledge ceases at a certain stage of life is a great illusion. Man needs to evolve through continuous learning throughout his life.

As children, our education and learning are done by our parents and teachers and we are obliged to accept them as absolute truths and the authority of both is not questioned.

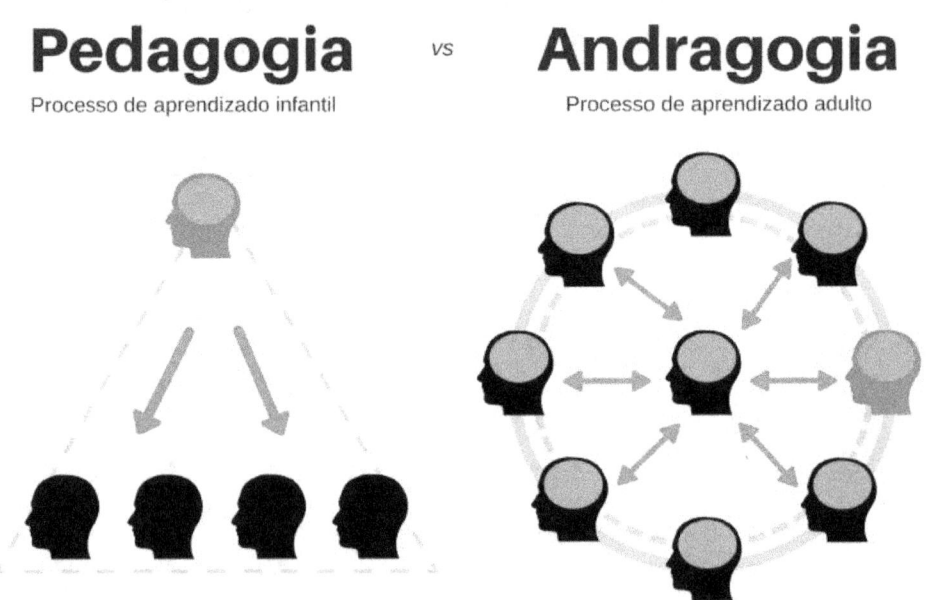

Figure 56 – Pedagogy Vs Andragogy.

In adolescence, this begins to change. Everything that is imposed is no longer accepted. Everything becomes questionable. The young man begins to rebel and the "umbilical cord" is broken. The authority of parents and teachers is already questioned and, at school, the student wants to know why he should learn this or that subject.

In adulthood, one becomes more mature and independent. Our free will and beliefs become responsible for our choices. This brings the adult living experiences where he learns from his own mistakes and successes. He is aware of what he does not know and how much this lack of knowledge is needed.

Andragogy is the science and art of adult education, while Pedagogy is the art and science of educating children and adolescents. Both form the basis of Anthropology, that is, the art and science of permanently educating human beings at any stage of their psychological development as a function of their cultural, ecological and social life.

However, the evolution of the human being has not yet been perceived by numerous educational institutions, as far as education is concerned. Schools and universities still apply the same teaching techniques to adults as they do in primary and secondary schools.

Perhaps this is the reason why you, dear reader, participate in countless refresher courses, workshops, congresses and events and get the impression that you left the same way you entered, that is, in the same way, without the event having brought you anything significant for immediate application in your work or in your profession.

This fact was noticed by Lindeman who wrote: "... Adult education will be through situations and not disciplines. Our academic system grows in reverse order: subjects and teachers constitute the educational axis. In conventional education, the student is required to conform to the established curriculum: in adult education, the curriculum is constituted according to the student's needs. Materials should only be introduced when necessary. Texts and teachers play a secondary role in this type of education; they must give the utmost importance to the apprentice."

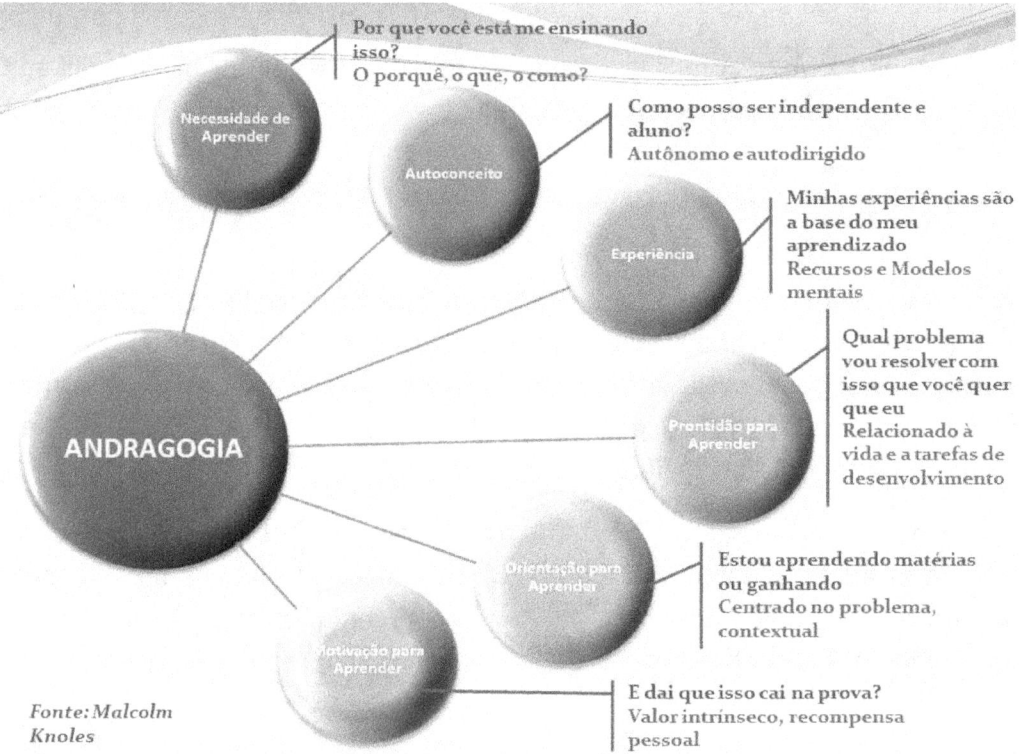

Figure 57 – Andragogy.

For more, the author continues: "... the most valuable force in adult education is the experience of the learner," and ends by stating: "Authoritarian teaching, exams that predetermine original thought, rigid pedagogical formulas – all these have no place in adult education. Adults who want to keep their minds fresh and vigorous begin to learn through the conflict of situations. They seek their references in the reservoirs of their experiences, even before the sources of secondary texts and facts. They are led to discussions by teachers, who are also references of knowledge and not oracles."

According to Knowles, as people become adults and mature, they undergo transformations, such as:

- They become self-directed, independent individuals.

- They accumulate life experiences that will be the foundation and substrate of their future learning.
- Her interest in learning is directed towards the development of skills that she uses in her social role, in her profession.
- They come to expect an immediate practical application of what they have learned, reducing their interest in knowledge that will be useful in the future.

For this reason, the characteristics of learning in Pedagogy and Andragogy are different, as we can see in the table below.

Features of the apprenticeship	Pedagogy	Andragogy
Teacher/student ratio.	Teacher is the center of actions, decides what to teach, how to teach and evaluate learning.	Learning acquires a more student-centred characteristic, independence and self-management of learning.
Reasons for learning.	Children and adolescents should learn what society expects them to know, following a standardized curriculum.	People learn what they really need to know (learning for practical application in daily life).
Motivation.	Motivation for learning is fundamentally the result of stimuli external to the student, such as grades, school grades, and teacher appreciation.	Adults are sensitive to external stimuli (grades, etc.), but it is internal factors that motivate them to learn (satisfaction, self-esteem, quality of life, etc.).
Student experience.	Teaching is didactic, standardized, and the student experience has little value.	Experience is a rich source of learning, through discussion and problem-solving done in groups.
Learning guidance.	Learning by subject or subject.	Problem-based learning, requiring a wide range of knowledge to reach the solution.

Willingness to learn.	The aim is to succeed and progress in school.	Adults are willing to start a learning process as long as they understand its usefulness to better face real problems in their personal and professional lives.

Table 2 - Learning characteristics.

It is clear that in the andragogical activity the cultural, professional and social point of view is the confrontation of experiences of two adults, the one who educates (facilitator) and the one who is educated (learner). The difference between the two disappears, since they are adults with experiences and equaled in the dynamic process of society.

In Andragogy, the traditional concept, where one teaches and the other learns, one knows and the other does not know, theoretically ceases to exist to become a reciprocal action where, often, the facilitator (teacher) is the one who learns.

The teacher needs to be humble enough to, in addition to becoming a learner, become an efficient tutor to demonstrate the practical importance of the subject to be studied; transmit enthusiasm for learning; show how that knowledge will make a difference in the lives of students; and, emphasize that that learning will change their lives and the lives of others.

If the teacher needs to change, the learner needs to start the process by changing their own values, their beliefs (unlearning in order to learn) and learning to be flexible, so that they increase their learning capacity. And this he will only achieve with a change in his attitudes.

All these principles are already being employed in firms, factories, etc., through the Human Relations departments. Administrative methods of TQC (total quality control) already foresee and take advantage of these characteristics of adults, who are stimulated, in periodic meetings, to discuss the problems in the different sectors and processes of their responsibility, their causes and possible solutions that will be implemented and reevaluated later.

We must not forget that colleges welcome teenagers as freshmen who will turn into adults at the end of the course. This implies that the work, during the undergraduate course, is on the border between Pedagogy and Andragogy.

Therefore, there should be a middle ground, where the positive characteristics of Pedagogy are preserved and the efficient innovations of Andragogy are introduced. The apprentice must have emphasized the need and training for continuous learning throughout his life, to become a more competent professional, with high self-esteem, sure of his abilities and committed to the society he will serve.

This is what will make this type of learning successful. While Pedagogy is one-way learning, Andragogy is two-way learning.

8.1 Andragogy in business

Andragogy, as we stated earlier, is the science and art of adult education, possessing basic characteristics that are totally different from Pedagogy.

Fundamentally, teaching is based on the exchange of experiences between two adults, the one who educates (facilitator) and the one who is educated (learner), both of whom are committed to solving problems of what they really need to know to apply in their daily lives.

Nowadays, an increasing number of people do not intend to stop working early. And, as the corporate world is a world in constant transformation, it can be inferred that as people age and continue to work longer, the greater the opportunities to continue learning constantly and continuously.

Man, by his very nature, can continue to learn throughout his life. And it is this continuous learning that will produce modifications, even in full old age, of their beliefs, customs, habits and opinions. That is why adults have more "life experience" than younger people, both in number and diversity.

Figure 58 – Andragogy.

Older people, when forming groups, show a unique heterogeneity with regard to their knowledge, interests, needs, etc. For andragogical teaching, this is a unique opportunity as this group becomes a living source for consultations and exchange of experiences. And all of this can and should be explored by group members through discussions, simulations, case presentations, etc., i.e. problem-based learning.

Therefore, the role of the teacher (facilitator) is fundamental. He needs to show the students (learners) the importance of the subject and approach it enthusiastically. It must show that it is important and that it will make a difference in their lives, changing it for the better both in their personal and professional aspects.

In andragogical teaching, another key factor is motivation. Especially in corporations, motivation is stimulated by external factors such as awards, promotion prospects, etc. However, the most striking and intense motivation comes from internal stimuli, because the adult learner will have more satisfaction for the work done, will have their self-esteem raised and, without a doubt, will improve their quality of life.

However, there are factors that can hinder, or even prevent, adult learning. Availability of time, access to libraries, laboratories, services, internet, etc., may be limiting factors in this learning. Therefore, companies that can make these items available will certainly contribute significantly to the success of the entire process.

8.2 Some basic principles

According to Ari B. de Oliveira, Andragogy has some basic principles:

- Sharing experiences is essential for adults, both to reinforce their beliefs and to influence the attitudes of others:
- The educational relationship of the adult is based between the facilitator and the learner, where both learn from each other, in an atmosphere of freedom and pro-action.
- The central focus is on learning, never teaching.
- Learning means acquiring knowledge, skill, and attitude.
- The learning process is developed in the following order: sensitization (motivation), research (study), discussion (clarification), experimentation (practice), conclusion (convergence) and sharing (sedimentation).
- Dialogue is the essence of the relationship: therefore, communication is only effective through it.
- Teacher (facilitator) and student (learner) share each other's knowledge with each other's experience. It is difficult to distinguish who learns more, the teacher or the student.
- The teacher needs to be humble enough to "come down from the pedestal of his chair" and situate himself on the same learning plane in order to, through sharing, develop together with the student.
- The student (learner) must be aware that he also needs to change his values and beliefs (learn to unlearn in order to relearn) and have more flexibility to increase his learning capacity.

- The learner must be motivated for lifelong learning, becoming, over the years, more competent, confident of his abilities and committed to the society in which he lives and serves.

Based on Miller's observation that "adults retain only 10% of what they hear after 72 hours, but are able to remember 85% of what they hear, see and do after the same 72 hours", it is clear that listening and doing become the fundamental procedures in adult learning.

All the principles mentioned above, according to Roberto de A. Cavalcanti, are already being used in the area of human resources "where management based on andragogical models replaces bureaucratic and hierarchical control, increasing commitment, self-esteem, responsibility and the ability of groups of employees to solve their problems at work".

For Rodrigo Goecks, "the andragogical concepts are being expanded to the areas of people management, strategic planning, marketing, communication, quality processes, etc. From simple meetings to complex strategic planning projects, they are following methods based on andragogical concepts.

Companies have already realized the advantages and have quickly implemented training programs to transform their employees into permanent facilitators within organizations."

In this way, all employees involved in the corporation's problems will seek solutions through meetings, exchange of ideas, description of personal experiences and experiences, simulations and presentation of cases in order to solve specific problems.

Nowadays, where competitiveness and productivity are the words of the hour, corporations need to be increasingly prepared, which implies the need for constant learning of their employees. And it is within this context that andragogical practices play a fundamental role. And where the profile of leaders and the role of leadership fit in.

This should be the role of the new leader, to be responsible for the learning of his team members; a person who can understand and accelerate learning and, at the same time, encourage and integrate the thinking of its members and get the best out of them for the benefit of all.

Stephen Covey (7), author of *the 8th Habit - From Effectiveness to Greatness,* states that we learn best when we teach someone else and that the best way to make people learn is to turn them into teachers, that is, each learner becomes a teacher and each teacher, a learner.

This behavior, when teaching or sharing what we learn with others, leads us, implicitly, to make a commitment to live what we have learned. And this "is the basis for deepening learning, dedication and motivation, making the change legitimate and engaging the support of the team", as Covey also states (7).

8.3 HR Administration

Many corporations, through their HR departments, are already realizing that a management based on an andragogical model brings advantages such as: replacement of bureaucratic and hierarchical control, greater commitment, increased self-esteem and increased responsibility and ability of their employees (alone or in groups) to achieve solutions to their problems for a better performance of their activities.

With this conduct, employees are stimulated in periodic meetings where problems are discussed, their causes are sought, possible solutions to be implemented or implemented are researched and, finally, reevaluated *a posteriori* at periodic intervals.

And it will be in this climate that people will seek, in their own experiences and in other sources, the construction of new knowledge for the solution of their problems.

8.4 Clash of generations

There is a current tendency for corporations to select younger employees, who, due to their performance, may assume leadership positions even before they turn thirty years old.

Although the figures indicate that 41% of executive positions are made up of people between 46 and 55 years old, 7% of this contingent is represented by professionals between the ages of 25 and 35.

What may represent for these young people a higher salary and other type of *status*, can also present negative aspects when it comes to leading and relating to older subordinates. On the other hand, older people may not surrender to a younger boss, either out of prejudice or rebellion.

In this type of situation, the question is: how to live together harmoniously?

The answer may lie in Andragogy. In other words, the young, daring and with new ideas, would be the receiver of the experiences of the older ones and these, in turn, would be the apprentices of what the younger one would be bringing to his company.

If the younger boss took over last week, it's only fair that the older ones should make him aware of everything that is necessary for the good performance and growth of the entire team. The youngest, on the other hand, will enrich the team with new ideas and new challenges that must also be shared in search of solutions and where everyone, team and company, profit together.

The boss, the leader, regardless of his age, must win the trust of his subordinates, try to get to know each one, maintain constant dialogues with all members of the team and, all together, establish the required action plans.

Learning from each other becomes the watchword in these cases, regardless of the position and age of each of the team members. And this relationship will constitute a living example of Andragogy.

Man needs to have a posture of constant learning, a learning that does not end at school or college, but is a constant action throughout life.

In short: learning are always words that move the corporate world and the personal "world" of each human being.

Leonardo Da Vinci said: "Learning is the only thing that the mind never tires of, is never afraid of, and never regrets."

Finally, let us always keep in mind the teaching of Erasmus of Rotterdam, a Dutch philosopher who lived between 1466 and 1536, who said: "reciprocal love between the one who learns and the one who teaches is the first and most important step to reach knowledge".

"The true value of human capital lies in its ability to adapt, learn and grow along with market changes, making it a competitive advantage for organizations."

Fonte: Gartner

9 CONCLUSION.

Formal learning and development programs that prepare employees for future roles are part of this, but it's difficult to make them effective.

Companies that are true learning organizations build their own formulas, customized to their needs.

We all go through a shift in our priorities and an adjustment of our ideals. People appreciate it when you have the flexibility to schedule your child or elderly parent so they can be there.

They are looking for a place where their humanity is appreciated, and they are more than a number. Encourage time and do everything in your power to provide a flexible schedule in an area that requires adequate coverage, the problem on the table, and urge your team to identify the planning challenge. They may have unique ideas that you haven't thought of yet.

Figure 59 – The Value of Human Capital.

It's inherently human that someone needs to feel meaningful, respected, wanted, and appreciated. Employees who feel important tend to work harder and stay with the organization longer.

At work, feeling important and meaningful is essential for enjoyment and motivation.

They are usually cheerful and go above and beyond.

Figure 60 – Dilbert and the corporate world.

10 FAQ.

1. Why is valuing human capital important for companies?

Valuing human capital is essential for companies because employees are considered one of the organization's main assets, contributing directly to productivity, innovation and competitiveness in the market.

2. What are the benefits of investing in employee development and training?

Investing in employee development and training can result in increased motivation, engagement, job satisfaction, talent retention, and improved individual and organizational performance.

3. How does valuing human capital impact organizational culture?

Valuing human capital can positively impact organizational culture, promoting collaboration, respect, diversity, innovation, and building a healthy and motivating work environment.

4. How does the valorization of human capital influence the company's image and reputation?

Valuing human capital can contribute to a positive image of the company in the eyes of employees, customers and society, demonstrating a commitment to people's well-being and development.

5. What strategies can companies adopt to value human capital?

Companies can adopt strategies such as leadership development programs, personalized training, constructive feedback, employee recognition, and fostering an inclusive and collaborative work environment.

6. How can valuing human capital contribute to talent retention?

When employees feel valued and recognized, they are more likely to stay with the company, reducing the turnover rate and the need to recruit and train new employees.

7. What is the role of leaders and managers in valuing human capital?

Leaders and managers play a key role in valuing human capital, being responsible for promoting a positive work environment, offering support, feedback and development opportunities to employees.

8. How is the valuation of human capital aligned with the company's business strategy?

Valuing human capital is aligned with the company's business strategy when employee development and engagement actions are integrated with organizational objectives, contributing to the achievement of planned goals and results.

9. What indicators can be used to measure the impact of human capital valuation on companies?

Some indicators that can be used to measure the impact of valuing human capital on companies include employee productivity, retention rate, job satisfaction index, level of engagement, and overall organizational performance.

10. How can valuing human capital be a competitive advantage for companies?

Valuing human capital can be a competitive advantage for companies by providing an attractive work environment, with motivated, engaged, and trained employees, capable of driving innovation, the quality of products and services, and customer loyalty, giving the company an advantage in the market.

11. What are soft skills and why are they important for human capital in companies?

Soft skills are behavioral and emotional skills that directly influence employee interactions and performance. They are fundamental for human capital in companies, as they contribute to the development of healthy interpersonal relationships, effective communication, leadership, conflict resolution, and teamwork.

12. How can soft skills impact organizational culture and employee engagement?

Soft skills have the power to positively impact organizational culture by promoting empathy, respect, collaboration, and diversity. Employees who possess and develop their soft skills tend to be more engaged, contribute meaningfully to the team, and feel more connected to the company's values and goals.

13. What are examples of soft skills valued in the corporate environment?

Some examples of soft skills valued in the corporate environment include empathy, effective communication, critical thinking, problem-solving skills, adaptability, leadership skills, teamwork, creativity, and emotional intelligence.

14. How can soft skills contribute to employee productivity and efficiency?

Soft skills can contribute to employee productivity and efficiency by improving communication, facilitating problem-solving, promoting collaboration between teams, encouraging innovation, increasing the ability to adapt to change, and strengthening interpersonal relationships in the workplace.

15. How can soft skills be developed and improved by employees?

Soft skills can be developed and improved through training, coaching, feedback, practice, and self-knowledge. The development of soft skills requires continuous effort and dedication on the part of employees, who can benefit both professionally and personally.

16. What is the role of leaders and managers in promoting the appreciation of soft skills in the human capital of companies?

Leaders and managers play a key role in promoting the appreciation of soft skills in companies' human capital. They should encourage and recognize the importance of behavioral and emotional skills in employees, demonstrating a living example of the value of these competencies in the workplace.

17. How can soft skills be a competitive differentiator for companies in today's market?

Soft skills can be a competitive differentiator for companies in today's market, as employees with skills such as effective communication, empathy, conflict resolution, and leadership are able to deal with challenges more effectively, contributing to innovation, productivity, and customer satisfaction.

18. What are the benefits of having employees with strong soft skills development?

The benefits of having employees with strong soft skills development include improving internal and external communication, building healthier interpersonal relationships, increasing effectiveness in problem-solving, fostering a collaborative work environment, and reducing conflict.

19. How can soft skills be assessed and integrated into employee selection and development processes?

Soft skills can be assessed through behavioral interviews, psychological tests, feedback from peers and managers, among other tools. In addition, companies can integrate soft skills into selection processes, performance appraisal, and professional development programs.

20. What is the importance of fostering the continuous development of soft skills among employees?

Fostering the continuous development of soft skills among employees is essential to keep up with market demands, adapt to new challenges, promote a collaborative and innovative work environment, and stand out as complete and competent professionals in today's job market.

21. What differentiates andragogy from pedagogy?

Andragogy is the teaching approach aimed at adults, while pedagogy is aimed at children and adolescents. Andragogy considers the experiences, motivations, and needs of adults, promoting autonomy and self-responsibility in the learning process.

22. What are the basic principles of andragogy?

Some basic tenets of andragogy include valuing the experience of adults, encouraging self-direction in learning, the immediate application of knowledge, respecting each individual's pace and learning style, and collaboration between students and teachers.

23. How can andragogy be applied in the corporate environment?

Andragogy can be applied in the corporate environment through training and development programs aimed at adults, which consider previous experiences, individual needs and the demands of the labor market, promoting meaningful and applicable learning.

24. What are effective teaching strategies based on andragogy?

Effective teaching strategies based on andragogy include promoting the active participation of students, applying case studies, encouraging reflection and discussion, valuing collaborative learning, and using educational technologies.

25. How can andragogy contribute to the professional development of adults?

Andragogy contributes to the professional development of adults by promoting more autonomous, relevant and meaningful learning, which allows the immediate application of knowledge in the work environment, favoring the personal and professional growth of individuals.

26. What are the challenges encountered in the application of andragogy in the educational context?

Some challenges encountered in the application of andragogy in the educational context include resistance to changing traditional educational paradigms, the adaptation of teachers and educational institutions to the new learning model, the personalization of teaching to meet the individual needs of adults, and the effective integration of technologies into the teaching and learning process.

27. What is the role of the teacher in the andragogical approach?

The role of the teacher in the andragogical approach is that of a facilitator of the learning process, acting as a guide, mediator and supporter of adults in their educational path. The teacher encourages reflection, autonomy and engagement of students, promoting a collaborative and meaningful learning environment.

28. How can andragogy promote the motivation of adults in the learning process?

Andragogy promotes the motivation of adults in the learning process by recognizing and valuing their individual experiences, needs and goals, providing personalized teaching, relevant and applicable to their professional and personal reality, which stimulates engagement and perseverance in the search for knowledge.

29. How can andragogy be applied in distance learning?

Andragogy can be applied in distance learning through interactive educational platforms, personalized content, active teaching methodologies, discussion forums, and collaborative activities, which promote autonomy, self-management, and meaningful learning in adults, regardless of physical distance.

30. What are the benefits of applying andragogy in higher education?

The benefits of applying andragogy in higher education include promoting students' self-confidence and self-responsibility, developing critical and reflective skills, applying academic knowledge in practice, and preparing students to

HUMAN CAPITAL AT WORK

10 REFERENCES.

ANDERLA, G. (1979). A informação em 1985. Rio de Janeiro: CNPq/IBICT, 1979.

ANTON, A. I., McCRACKEN, W. M., POTTS, C., 1994. "Goal Decomposition and Scenario Analysis in Business Process Reengineering". In: Proceedings of the 6th International Conference on Advanced Information Systems Engineering (CAiSE'94), Springer, Utrecht, NL (Jun), pp. 94-104.

ARAUJO, V.M.R.H. de. (1991). Informação: instrumento de dominação e de submissão. Revista Ciência da Informação, v. 20, n. 1, p. 37-44, jan./jun.

ARAUJO, V.M.R.H. de. (1995) Sistemas de Informação: nova abordagem teórico conceitual. Revista Ciência da Informação, v. 24, n. 1, p. 37-44.

ÁVILA, Thiago J. T. 2015. Uma proposta de modelo de processo para publica‚c~ao de Dados Abertos Conectados Governamentais. Disponível em: http://www.consultaesic.cgu.gov.br/busca/dados/Lists/Pedido/Attachments/571437/RESPOSTA_PEDIDO_Thiago%20Avila%20-%20Dissertao%20-%20PPGMCC.pdf. Acesso em 12 dez.2019.

BARRETO, A. A. (1996) Eficiência técnica e econômica e a viabilidade de produtos e serviços de informação. Revista Ciência da Informação, v.25. n.3, p.405-414, set/dez.

BAUMAN, Zygmunt. Vida para Consumo: a transformação das pessoas em mercadoria. Rio de Janeiro: Zahar, 2008.

BELKIN, N.J. (1978). Information concepts for information science. Journal of Documentation, v. 34, n. 1, p. 55-85.

BELKIN, N.J., ROBERTSON, S.E. (1976) Information science and the phenomenon of information. Jasis, v.27, n.4, p.197-204.

BELL, T. E., THAYER, T. A., 1976. "Software Requirements: Are They Really a Problem?". In: Proceedings of International Conference on Software Engineering (ICSE-2), San Francisco, CA, pp. 61-68.

BIARNÈS, Jean. Universalité, Diversité e Sujet dans l'espace Pédagogique. Paris: L'Harmattan, 1999.

BOURDIEU, Pierre. Excluídos do Interior. In: NOGUEIRA, Maria Alice; CATANI, Afrânio (Org.). Escritos de Educação. [S.l.:s.n.], 1998. P. 217-227.

BRETON, P. & PROULX S. (1989). L'explosion de la communication. la naissance d'une nouvelle idéologie. Paris: La Découverte.

BUBENKO, J. A., WANGLER, B., 1993. "Objectives Driven Capture of Business Rules and of Information System Requirements". IEEE Systems Man and Cybernetics'93 Conference, Le Touquet, France.

BUENO, Maria Sylvia Simões. Políticas Atuais para o Ensino Médio. Campinas: Papirus, 2000.

CASTRO, J., KOLP, M., MYLOPOULOS, J., 2002. "Towards Requirements-Driven Information Systems Engineering: The TROPOS Project". Information Systems 27(6): 365-389.

CASTRO, J.; KOLP, M.; MYLOPOULOS, J., 2001. "A requirements-driven development methodology". In: Proceedings of the 13th International Conference on Advanced Information Systems Engineering (CAiSE-01), Interlaken, Switzerland.

CAVALCANTI, R. A. Andragogia: a aprendizagem nos adultos. Disponível em: http://www.rau-tu.unicamp.br/nou-rau/ead/documentt/view=2

CHARLOT, Bernard. Da Relação com o Saber: elementos para uma teoria. Porto Alegre: Artmed, 2000.

CHARLOT, Bernard. Relação com o Saber, Formação dos Professores e Globalização: questões para a educação hoje. Porto Alegre: Artmed, 2005. CHARLOT, Bernard. A Relação com o Saber nos Meios Populares: uma investigação nos Liceus profissionais no subúrbio. Portugal: Legis Editora, 2009a. CHARLOT, Bernard. A Escola e o Trabalho dos Alunos. Sísifo. Revista de Ciências da Educação, São Paulo, n. 10, p. 89-96, 2009b.

CHERRY, C. (1974) A comunicação humana. São Paulo: Cultrix, Ed. da USP.

CHUNG, L., NIXON, B., YU, E., MYLOPOULOS, J., 2000. Non-Functional Requirements in Software Engineering. Kluwer Publishing.

CIAVATTA, Maria (Org.). Ensino Médio: ciência, cultura e trabalho. Brasília: Secretaria da Educação Média e Tecnológica/MEC/SEMTEC, 2004. P. 73-91. SPOSITO, Marília;

COMPUTER, 1985. Special Issue on Requirements Engineering, IEEE Computer.

COSTA, Marisa Vorraber. Entrevista realizada por Francisco Eboli com RAMOS DO Ó, Jorge e com COSTA, Marisa Vorraber. Desafios à escola contemporânea: um diálogo. Revista Educação e Realidade, Porto Alegre, v. 32, n. 2, p. 109-116, jul./dez. 2007.

COVEY, S.R. – O 8º hábito. Da eficácia à grandeza. Rio de Janeiro, Elsevier, 2005.

CYSNEIROS, L. M., LEITE, J., 2001. "Using the Language Extended LExicon to Support NFR Elicitation". In: Proceedings of the 5th Workshop on Requirements Engineering, Buenos Aires, Argentina (Nov).

DARDENNE, A., VAN LAMSWEERDE, A., FICKAS, S., 1993. "Goal Directed Requirements Acquisition". Science of Computer Programming, 20, pp.3-50.

DAVIES, T. 2010. Open data, democracy and public sector reform. Dissertação – University of Oxford, Oxford. Disponível em: http://www.opendataimpacts.net/report/. Acesso em 29 nov. 2019.

DOBSON, J. S., 1992. "A Methodology for Managing Organizational Requirements". University of Newcastle upon Tyne, UK.

DORFMAN, M., THAYER, R. H., 1990. Standards, Guidelines and Examples of System and Software Requirements Engineering. Los Alamitos, CA, IEEE Computer Society Press.

DOURADO, Luiz Fernandes; OLIVEIRA, João Ferreira de. A Qualidade da Educação: perspectivas e desafios. Caderno CEDES [online], Campinas, v. 29, n. 78, p. 201-215, 2009.

DRUCKER, P. (1993) Post-capitalist society. Harder Business, New York.

DRUCKER, Peter. (1995). Administrando tempos de grandes mudanças. São Paulo: Ed. Pioneira, Cap.12 As informações que os executivos necessitam, p.75-89.

ELMASRI, R.; WUU, Gene T. J.; KORAMAJIAN, Vram. 1993. A Temporal Model and Query Language for EER Databases. In: Tansel, A. et al. Temporal Databases: theory, designs and implementation. Redwood City: The Benjamim/Cummings Publishing, p.212-229.

ELMASRI, R; KOURAMA-JIAN, Vram. 1992. A Temporal Query Language Based on Conceptual Entities and Roles. In International Conference on the Entity Relationship Approach, 11, 1992, Karlsruhe, Germany. Proccedings Berlin: Springer Verlag, p.375-388. (Lecture Notes in Computer Science, v.645).

FERG, S. 1985. Modeling the Time Dimension in an Entity-Relationship Diagram. In 4th International Conference on the Entity-Relationship Approach, p. 200-286, Silver Spring, MD. Computer Society Press.

GALVÃO, Izabel. A Experiência e as Percepções de Jovens na Vida Escolar na Encruzilhada das Aprendizagens: o conhecimento, a indisciplina, a violência. Perspectiva, Florianópolis, v. 22, n. 02, p. 345-380, jul./dez. 2004.

GAUCHET, Marcel. Les Sens des Savoirs en Question. Conferência apresentada no dia 7 nov. 2005. <http://www.diffusion.ens.fr/index>. Acesso em: 3 abr. 2006.

GOECKS, R. – Educação de adultos – Uma abordagem andragógica. Disponível em: www.serprofessoruniversitario.pro.br/ler.php?modulo=18texto=4

HEILPRIN, L. B. (1989) Foundations of Information Science reexamined. Annual Review of Information Science and Technology, v.24, p. 343-372.

HELBIG C, RINK K, Marx A, PRIESS J, FRANK M, KOLDITZ O (2012) Visual integration of diverse environmental data : a case study in Central Germany. In: Proceedings of iEMSs Conference 2012, Leipzig, Germany, pp 1–8 http://www.serprofessoruniversitario.pro.br/ler.php?modulo=18texto=4

IEEE, 1984. IEEE Std. 830 - IEEE Guide to Software Requirements Specification. The Institute of Electrical and Electronics Engineers, New York, USA.

IEEE, 1998. IEEE/ANSI 830-1998, Recommended Practice for Software Requirements Specifications, IEEE, NY. In: Proceedings of the 22nd International Conference on Software Engineering (ICSE), Limerick, Ireland (Jun).

JACKSON, M., 1995. Software Requirements and Specifications: A Lexicon of Practice.

JACOBSON, I., 1992. Object Oriented Software Engineering: A Use Case Driven Approach. Addison-Wesley, New York.

JARVELIN, K. & VAKKARI, P. (1993) The evolution of Library and Information Science 1965-1985: a content analysis of journal articles. Information Processing & Management, v.29, n.1, p. 129-144.

KETTL, Donald. (1996), The Global Revolution. Trabalho apresentado no seminário Reforma do Estado na América Latina e no Caribe. MARE/BID/ONU, Brasilia.

KING, W. R., GROVER, V., HUFNAGEL, E. H. (1989) Using information and information technology for sustainable competitive advantage: some emprirical evidence. Information & Management, 17.

KLOPPROGGE, M. R. 1981. TERM: An Approach to Include the Time Dimension in the Entity-Relationship Model. In Proceedings of the Second International Conference on the Entity Relationship Approach, p. 477-512, Washington, DC.

KNOWLES, M. – The adult learner: a neglected species.3 rd. ed., Houston, New Republic, 1984.

KOTONYA, G., SOMMERVILLE, I., 1997. Requirements Engineering: Processes and Techniques. Wiley, John & Sons Inc.

KRAWCZYK, Nora. Desafios do Ensino Médio no Brasil hoje. Cadernos de Pesquisa, São Paulo, v. 41, n. 144, p. 752-769, set./dez. 2011. KUENZER, Acácia Zeneida (Org.). Ensino Médio: construindo uma proposta para os que vivem do trabalho. São Paulo: Cortez, 2000.

KRAWCZYK, Nora; ZIBAS, Dagmar. Reforma do Ensino Médio no Brasil: seguindo tendências ou construindo novos caminhos? Revista Educação Brasileira, Brasília, v. 23, n. 47, p. 83-102, jul./dez., 2001.

LEFFINGWELL, D., WIDRIG, D., 2000. Managing Software Requirements: A Unified Approach. G. Booch, I. Jacobson, J. Rumbaugh (eds.) The Object Technology Series, Addison-Wesley, NY.

LEITÃO, D.M. (1993) A informação como insumo estratégico. Ciência da Informação, Brasília, v.22, n.2, p.118-123, maio/ago.

LEITE, J., et al., 1997. "Enhancing a Requirements Baseline with Scenarios". In: proceedings of the Third IEEE International Symposium on Requirements Engineering, IEEE Computer Society Press, Los Alamitos, CA, USA, pp. 44-53.

LINDERMAN, E.C. – The meaning of adult education. New York, New republic, 1926.

LOUCOPOULOS, P., KARAKOSTAS, V., 1995. System Requirements Engineering, McGraw-Hill, London.

LOUCOPOULOS, P., KATSOULI, E., 1992. Modelling Business Rules in an Office Environment. ACM SIGOIS (Aug).

LOUCOPOULOS, P.; THEODOULIDIS, C.; WANGLER, B. 1991. The Entity Relationship Time Model and Conceptual Rule Language. In International Conference on the Entity Relationship Approach, 10, San Mateo, California.

MACAULAY, L. A., 1996. Requirements Engineering. Springer, London. Referências MacDONALD, I. G., 1986. "Information Engineering". In: Olle T. W., Sol H. G., e Verrijn- Stuart A. A. (eds.) Information System Design Methodologies: Improving the Practice, Elsevier/North Holland, Amsterdam.

MACEDO, N., LEITE, J., 1999. "Elicit@99: Um Protótipo de Ferramenta para a Elicitação de Requisitos". In: Proceedings of the II (Ibero-American) Workshop on Requirements Engineering (WER99), Buenos Aires, Argentina (Sep).

MACHADO, Felipe Nery Rodrigues, Projeto de Banco de Dados: uma visão prática/Felipe Nery Rodrigues Machado, Maurício Pereira de Abreu, São Paulo, Editora Erica, 1996. (Livro texto)

MACHADO, Felipe Nery Rodrigues. 2018. Banco de Dados-Projeto e Implementação. [S.l.]: Editora Saraiva.

MACHADO, Nilson José. Conhecimento e Valor. São Paulo: Moderna editora, 2004.

MAIDEN, N., 1998. "CREWS-SAVRE: Scenarios for Acquiring and Validating Requirements". Automated Software Engineering, 5(4): 419-446.

MANYIKA, J.; et al. 2013. Open data: Unlocking innovation and performance with liquid information. Mackinsey & Company, Londres. Disponível em: http://www.mckinsey.com/insights/business_technology/open_data_unlocking_innovation_and_performance_with_liquid_information.

McDERMID, J., 1994. "Requirements Analysis: Orthodoxy, Fundamentalism and Heresy". In: Jirotka M. e Goguen J. A. (eds.) Requirements Engineering: Social and Technical Issues, Academic Press, London, pp. 17-40.

MENEZES, Luís Carlos de. O Novo Público e a Nova Natureza do Ensino Médio. Estudos Avançados, São Paulo, v. 15, n. 42, p. 201-208, 2001. RAMOS DO Ó, Jorge. Entrevista realizada por Francisco Eboli com RAMOS DO Ó, Jorge e com COSTA, Marisa Vorraber. Desafios à escola contemporânea: um diálogo. Revista Educação e Realidade, Porto Alegre, v. 32, n. 2, p. 109-116, jul./ dez. 2007.

MERCURIO, V., MEYERS, B. F., NISBET, A. M., RADIN, G., 1990. AD/Cycle Strategy and Architecture. IBM Systems Journal, 29(2).

MEYER, Bertrand. Object-Oriented Software Construction. Prentice-Hall,1997.

MILLER K. – In: GOECKS, R. – Educação de adultos – Uma abordagem andragógica.

MYLOPOULOS, J., CHUNG, L., LIAO, S., WANG, H., YU, E., 2001. "Exploring Alternatives during Requirements Analysis". IEEE Software (Jan/Feb), pp. 2-6.

MYLOPOULOS, J., CHUNG, L., NIXON, B., 1992. "Representing and Using Non-Functional Requirements: A Process-Oriented Approach". IEEE Transactions on Software Engineering, Vol. 18, No. 6 (Jun), pp. 483-497.

NELLBORN, C., BUBENKO, J., GUSTAFSSON, M., 1992. "Enterprise Modelling – The Key to Capturing Requirements for Information Systems". Deliverable 3-1-3-R1,

NUSEIBEH, B., EASTERBROOK, S., 2000. "Requirements Engineering: A Roadmap".

OLIVEIRA, A.B. – Andragogia – A educação de adultos. Disponível em: www.geocities.com/sjuvella/andragogia.html

PERSIVAL, I. (1992). Chaos: a science for the real world. In: Hall, N. (ed.) The new scientist guide to chaos. London: Penguin Books.

POHL, K., 1993. "The Three Dimensions of Requirements Engineering". In: Rolland C., Bodart F., Cauvet C. (eds.) 5th International Conference on Advanced Information Systems Engineering (CAiSE'93), Springer-Verlag, Paris, pp. 275-292.

PRIETO-DIAZ, R., 1990. "Domain Analysis: An Introduction". ACM SIGSOFT, Software Engineering Notes, Vol. 15, No. 2 (Apr), pp. 47-54.

ROBINSON, R., 1996. "Put The Rapid Into RAD". Datamation, Vol. 42, No. 4 (Feb), 80(1).

RUMBAUGH, J. et al., 1991. Object-Oriented Modeling and Design. First Edition, Prentice Hall, Englewood Cliffs, NJ, 1991.

SANTOS, Cleber N. Políticas da Educação a Distância no Ensino Superior: o foco no aluno do Sistema UAB/UFAL. Maceió: UFAL, 2011. 315 f. Dissertação (Mestrado em Educação) – Programa de Pós-Graduação em Educação Brasileira, Centro de Educação, Universidade Federal de Alagoas, Maceió, 2011.

SANTOS, Jair Ferreira dos. O que é Pós-moderno. São Paulo: Brasiliense, 1995.

SCHNEIDER, G., WINTERS, J., 1998. Applying Use Cases: A Practical Guide. Addison-Wesley, New York.

SHAW, M., GAINES, B., 1995. "Requirements Acquisition". Software Engineering Journal, vol. 11.

SHERA, J. H. & Cleveland, D. B. (1977). History and foundations of Information Science. Annual Review of Information Science and Technology, v. 12, p.248-275.

SILVA, Maria Abádia da. Qualidade Social da Educação Pública: algumas aproximações. Caderno CEDES [online], Campinas, v. 29, n. 78, p. 216-226, 2009. Educação & Realidade, Porto Alegre, v. 39, n. 4, p. 1185-1207, out./dez. 2014. Disponível em: Reis 1207

SNODGRASS, r. 1985. A Temporal Query Language. In Conference: Proceedings of the 1985 ACM SIGMOD International Conference on Management of Data, Austin, Texas, May 28-31, 1985. Disponível em:

https://pdfs.semanticscholar.org/e6a7/3129290b9b2fbd7b3c4bdb38d5515aedbde9.pdf. Acesso em 04 dez. 2019.

SOLTYS, R., CRAWFORD, A., 1999. "JAD for Business Plans and Designs". http://www.thefacilitator.com/htdocs/article11.html

SOMMERVILLE, I., 2007. Software Engineering. Eigth Edition, Addison Wesley.

SPOSITO, Marília. Uma Perspectiva Não Escolar no Estudo Sociológico da Escola. Revista USP, São Paulo, n. 57, p. 210-226, mar./maio 2003.

TAUZOVICH, Branka. 1991. Towards Temporal Extensions to the Entity Relationship Approach, San Mateo, California.

TORANZO, M. A., 2002. "Uma Proposta para Melhorar o Rastreamento de Requisitos de Software". Centro de Informática, Universidade Federal de Pernambuco, Tese de Doutorado, Dezembro/2002.

UBALDI, B. 2013. Open Government Data: Towards empirical analysis of open government data iniciatives. OECD Working Papers on Public Governance, nº 22. Disponível em: http://dx.doi.org/10.1787/5k46bj4f03s7-en. Acesso em: 06 mar. 2019.

VAN LAMSWEERDE, A., 2000. "Requirements Engineering in the year 00: A Research Perspective". In: Proceedings of the 22nd International Conference on Software Engineering (ICSE), Limerick, Ireland (Jun).

VAN LAMSWEERDE, A., DARDENNE, A., DUBISY, F., 1991. "The KAOS Project: Knowledge Acquisition in Automated Specification of Software". In: Proceedings of the AAAI Spring Symposium Series, Stanford University (Mar).

VAN ZANTEN, Agnès. L'École de la Périphérie: scolarité et ségrégation en banlieue. Paris: Presses Universitaires de France, 2001.

VILLER, S., SOMMERVILLE, I., 1999. "Social Analysis in the Requirements Engineering Process: From Ethnography to Method". In: Proceedings of the 4th International Symposium on Requirements Engineering, Limerick, Ireland (Jun).

WELLER, Wivian. Grupos de Discussão na Pesquisa com Adolescentes e Jovens: aportes teórico-metodológicos e análise de uma experiência com o método. Educação e Pesquisa, São Paulo, v. 32, n. 2, p. 241-260, maio/ago., 2006.

WIERINGA, R. J., 1996. Requirements Engineering: Frameworks for Understanding. John Wiley e Sons, New York.

YU, E., 1995. "Modelling Strategic Relationships for Process Reengineering". Phd Thesis, University of Toronto.

YUEXIAO, C. (1988) Definitions and sciences of information. Information Processing & Management, v. 24, n. 4, p. 479-491.

ZAVE, P., 1997. Classification of Research Efforts in Requirements Engineering. ACM Computer Surveys, Vol. 29, No. 4.

ZEMAN, J. (1970) Significado filosófico da noção de informação. In: O conceito de informação na ciência contemporânea. Trad. Maria Helena Kühner. Rio de Janeiro: Paz e Terra.

ZIBAS, Dagmar M. L. O Ensino Médio na Voz de Alguns de seus Autores. São Paulo: FCC/DPE, 2001.

HUMAN CAPITAL AT WORK

"Every great dream begins with a dreamer. Always remember that you have within you the strength, patience and passion to reach for the stars to change the world."

Harriet Tubman

11 MEET THE AUTHOR.

11.1 Prof. Marcão - Marcus Vinícius Pinto.

Figure 61 - The Value of Human Capital.

In my career, which has been marked by decades of experience in information technology and marketing, it is important to highlight my constant search for improvement and a deep understanding of information science and the complex functioning of the human mind.

Despite the challenge of living with a physical disability, more specifically the absence of the left foot, this singular fact has driven me to constantly seek to overcome and value the uniqueness of each individual.

Currently, I'm in a moment of consolidation in my career as a writer. I am deeply involved with topics related to information science and seek to bring to light an insightful and comprehensive view of the complex processes of data storage, organization, and dissemination.

Through my words, I seek to unveil the complexities of the human being and his mind in all its nuances.

During these decades, I have dedicated myself intensively to information architecture, attribute engineering and software development projects, using different methodologies to ensure the efficiency and quality of the products I am proud to create.

I understand the importance of proposing methodologies that allow optimizing resources and improving the quality of database projects. In this sense, I highlight the data modeling and Data Warehouse standards, as well as the methodology for validating and managing data models, which are fundamental to achieve solid and reliable results.

In addition to acting as a business consultant, where I offer innovative solutions to complex problems and help organizations overcome challenges, I am also dedicated to sharing my knowledge through lectures, training, and mentoring of careers and business development.

At the same time, I am a content producer on YouTube, which allows me to disseminate ideas and dialogue with an audience eager for knowledge and innovation.

Throughout my career, I have had the privilege of publishing 32 books to date, all of which are available on Amazon's platform, providing access to a wide audience in search of in-depth knowledge and insights.

However, even though I am involved in all these professional activities, I never let go of my constant learning process, finding happiness in the little things and pursuing my true purposes of helping those who seek me.

I have a deep respect for everyone and dedicate myself to activities that transcend work, such as the study of the universe of music on the piano.

In addition, my personal life is also important to me. I have been married to my beloved wife, Andrea, since 1998, and our union is filled with happiness and companionship.

11.2 Some books published by Prof. Marcão.

11.3 Books on Open Data by Prof. Marcão.

Figure 62 – Some books by Prof. Marcão.

11.4 How to contact Prof. Marcão.

For lectures, training and business mentoring, please contact me on my LinkedIn profile or by email marcao.tecno@gmail.com.

It will be a pleasure to interact with you.

Prof. Marcão – MARCUS VINÍCIUS PINTO

CONSULTING | MENTORING | TRAINING | LECTURES

marcao.tecno@gmail.com

https://bit.ly/linkedin_profmarcao

Be my follower and get access to unmissable content!

Instagram: https://bit.ly/3tpZ5kp

YouTube: https://bit.ly/4ah44nT

Linkedin: https://bit.ly/linkedin_profmarcao

My Amazon Author Page: https://amzn.to/3S2xCgL

Spotify: https://spoti.fi/3c0fClN

Linktree: https://linktr.ee/tudo_prof.marcao

MY CONSULTING FIRM: https://mvpconsult.com.br/

> With so much technology, teachers will be more valued as trainers of reasoning, ethics, and citizenship. You see? There is no artificial intelligence for that.
>
> *Prof. Marcão*

Figure 63 – Let's value teachers.

www.ingramcontent.com/pod-product-compliance
Lightning Source LLC
Chambersburg PA
CBHW062102220526
45471CB00010B/3569